One River More

Books by W. D. Wetherell

Short Stories
The Man Who Loved Levittown
Hyannis Boat and Other Stories
Wherever That Great Heart May Be

Novels
Souvenirs
Chekhov's Sister
The Wisest Man in America

Essays
Vermont River
Upland Stream
North of Now

Travel
The Smithsonian Guide to the Natural Places of Northern New England

One River More

W. D. Wetherell

THE LYONS PRESS

Printed in the United States of America

10 9 8 7 6 5 4 3 2 1

Design by Joel Friedlander, Marin Bookworks

Library of Congress Cataloging-in-Publication Data
Wetherell, W. D.
    One river more/W. D. Wetherell.
      p. cm.
      1. Fly fishing—Anecdotes. 2. Rivers—Anecdotes. 3.
  Wetherell, W. D. I. Title.
    SH456.W373   1998
    799.1'757'092—dc21   98-9180
                                CIP

ISBN 1-55821-698-7 (trade edition)
ISBN 1-55821-750-9 (limited edition)
ISBN 1-55821-751-7 (deluxe edition)

For all the Tousignants

Contents

PART ONE

Early Days

The Waiting Game

EVERY FLY FISHER KNOWS there are two fishing seasons: the official one set by the fish and game department, and the richer, more fluid one set by your heart. In most northern states the first comes in mid-April, which is a joke for everyone except the worm fishermen, and with the streams so high and cloudy, not a particularly funny one even for them. The second starts—Well, take your pick. When the first tackle catalogs come in January, just when you're at your weakest, so spending money on equipment seems a plausible substitute for actually fishing? Sometime after Christmas when, using that new vise Santa brought, you tie up your first pattern for the coming year? When brochures are sent for from Montana, Alaska, Argentina, or, better yet, when a deposit is actually mailed? Everyone picks their date, and for me, though I've tried every psychological trick there is, every coaxing, I've never been able to get the season of expectation to open any sooner than the first week of March.

January and February, the long weeks leading up to the equinox. These are strictly working months here, the time I earn my fishing time, literally put it in the bank—and not only a real bank, but that more complex lending institution that revolves around family goodwill. When I do go outdoors it's usually to ski through the mixed softwoods that start behind our house, and the only thing this has to do with fishing is that occasionally I'll catch that low, throaty surge of water as I cross a frozen stream— a sound no river lover can hear without sensing a matching pulse coursing through their blood. I'll even try poking at the snow with my ski pole just to see if I can't liberate some watery brightness; once, doing this on a day of extreme cold, I pulled back out a perfect popsicle, my pole frozen from the tip over the basket into a clear blue ball of ice.

Other than these little foretastes, there's not much going on. The sun gets brighter, the days get longer, and if you wake up early enough you can see Vega and the summer constellations rising over the low mountains to our east like coming attractions scrolled over a dark orange screen. But when you live in northern New England as long as I have, you develop a little damper on your hope, try not to get excited. Another month until fishing is even a remote possibility; two months until I'll actually venture out; three months until hatches start and conditions become halfway decent; four months until the glory days of June and early July. It's simply too much hard time left in the sentence, so, like a prisoner facing freedom, I find it's better not to think about it at all.

If I do give in to temptation, it's still retrospectively; it's last year's fishing I'm remembering, getting out the pictures, glancing at my fishing calendar, taking solace from modest triumphs that have only been enhanced by the intervening months. I notice the same backward inclination in talking with my fishing partners. Meeting in January, we're still talking about *last* summer on the Yellowstone, not *next* summer on the Androscoggin.

As I said, all this changes around March first when I start

giving myself permission to think about the coming season. The winter seems endless at this stage, the storms we always get around town meeting day being among our most ferocious, and what robins or blackbirds manage to find their way up here are often blown right back to Massachusetts by the frigid northwest wind. But still, there's something in the air now—a vague earthy scent, little trills and whispers from meltwater, a growing confidence in the sun—that at least enables you to pronounce the word *spring*, not like a remote, half-imagined abstraction, but as a reality, the appearance of which won't be spooked by mentioning its name out loud.

In short, late winter is very much a waiting game, one every fly fisher has to play as best they can. There are time-honored means for doing so, of course, some of which I take part in, others I prefer to sit out. One of these is ice-fishing. Our local pond will have its little village of companionable shacks most winters, at least when the ice has a chance to thicken before being covered by an insulating blanket of snow. The fact I've never actually gotten up the energy to dig a hole, let a line down, hoist a flag shouldn't obscure the fact I can understand perfectly the motives of those doing so. The hard crystalline beauty of a frozen pond in winter; the polar bear companionship of people who are as thickly booted, mitted, and hatted as you are yourself; the restorative dashes back to the shed for whatever is in the thermos or flask. Dig me a trench, get a hatch started, oil a fly line with antifreeze, and I'd be out there in a second.

Fly tying is another form of winter fishing, one I have all the respect for in the world, but don't have the knack for and probably never shall. It's an art and a demanding one; Carrie Stevens, Helen Shaw, Roy Steenrod, the Darbees: these are great and honored names, and rightly so, for the skill these tyers bring to their work, the combination of preciseness and flair, experience

5

and imagination, can only be compared with the work of the great nature artists or the most skilled jewelers.

For me, those long hours hunched over a tying bench are a little too similar to the long hours hunched over a writing desk, a little too much for my back, eyes, and nerves to handle. But as something to tide you over between seasons, I don't see how it can be beat.

Neither ice fisherman nor fly tyer, I'm left with a lot of winter hours to fill, or at least would be if it wasn't for the fact there are plenty of other fishing surrogates, stopgaps, and pacifiers waiting on line. The following is a short list, both of the kinds of things I personally find helpful in waiting out March and suggestions for anyone faced with the same predicament.

1. FORM RESOLUTIONS.

I have this terrible habit I'm half-ashamed to admit: I'm the kind who keeps their New Year's resolutions. Of course this is absurdly anal of me, priggish, straight-arrowish to a fault, and wins me more suspicion and disgust than it does approbation. So I'm always careful with my resolves, since, as with wishes, they very well may come true.

I think I'm on safe ground this year, at least with fishing. For I've formed two resolutions, one on the practical side, one on the practical-spiritual.

The first is never to lose a fish this season through a badly tied knot. Adding an extra half-hitch when you tie on your fly; sitting down out of the wind and concentrating as you fashion a blood knot; checking the breaking strength of your tippets. In theory, these are the easiest preventatives in the world—and yet how tedious and slow that extra care can seem when actually fishing. The trout are rising, your hands are shaking from excitement or cold, you realize it's been a while since you last checked

6

connections, but. . . . No, it's simply one task too much, like getting back out of a warm, cozy bed to floss your teeth. Trout, of course, ask for nothing better, and will undo a bad knot with what always seems a particularly gleeful, tah-dah kind of flourish—trout as disappearing act, trout unbound.

The second resolution may be a little harder to keep, for all my self-discipline. Last year my friend Tom Ciardelli and I finished salmon season up in Maine, fishing the Rapid River for landlocks. What with logging roads going everywhere now, four-wheel drive and ATVs, the lower Rangeleys aren't as remote as they once were, and we had more company than either of us would have liked. So, with no alternative open, we pretty much stayed on one pool, the one neglected pool, the entire day.

This was something of a precedent for a fisherman who, like a salmon himself, always forges relentlessly upstream. A revelation, too, since I discovered how rewarding it can be to concentrate on one small stretch of river and yet concentrate on this intensely, getting to know it in all its moods—the different ways the sunlight comes off the water at dawn, midday, and dusk; the movement of fish within a pool, their feeding cycle so exuberantly on and so stubbornly off; insect emergence and how much life comes off the water if you have the patience to sit and watch. And narrowing the focus paid off in fish—we learned that too, sight-fishing for salmon who came up to small gray midges with interest, respect, and, finally, acceptance.

Hence my resolution. To slow it down this year, my fishing, my pace upstream. Not go chasing after the river, but, waiting patiently, to let the river come to me.

2. FIGHT THE GOOD FIGHT.

Conservation groups like to hold their annual banquets in March, the month when their members are unlikely to be off fishing and are most eager to hear a speaker wax informative on the subject. And while I'm not a banquet type of guy, I do try to send in money for raffle tickets, donate a book or two, help out where I can. If nothing else, the invitations that come in the mail are good reminders of something I think should become *the* off-season activity for all devoted fly fishers: working to make sure there is a trout stream to go back to when the snow disappears.

This winter several such campaigns have concerned me enough to warrant my involvement. Across the river in Vermont, trout fishers are fighting the ski industry again, this time over the industry's plans to loot water from headwater streams to use in snowmaking, and to make snow from treated wastewater (conservationists, prompted by this last folly, have bumper stickers reading *Effluent for the Affluent!*).

I've departed from my usual shyness about such things to go to a meeting on the subject, give a talk. At the same time, I'm talking to people here in town about saving a remote pond at the base of our local mountain. Grunt work mostly, stuffing envelopes, writing appeals, asking for donations. There's a land trust that owns it now, having obtained it in a complicated three-way trade, but they're holding it only temporarily, and it's up to the town to raise the funds to preserve it forever.

That's locally. Nationally, I'm distressed to read about the gold mine planned on the Blackfoot in Montana and on other mountain streams, the poisonous leachings and what they would do. With less of a direct role open for me, I've ponied up the fifty dollars for membership in a coalition fighting the threats, trying via this modest but necessary means to lend my support. Again, it feels meet and right to do so; when I wade into my own river this spring, I want to be able to look it in the eye.

3. PERUSE CATALOGS.

Not quite the off-season activity it used to be for me, since with great effort I've gotten past the acquisitive, tackle-mania stage everyone goes through at least once in their fishing career. Between a back-to-basics mind-set, a longing to continually simplify, a bank account that is always challenged, skimming through fishing catalogs has become mostly a spectator sport for me. Still, I spend some time at it, since the mail carries them in on a springtime freshet of gloss, hype, and exaggeration, and I'm still not immune to being swept along.

If nothing else, they're a good way to keep up with the state of the sport, what's in and what's out. Thus, going through this year's batch, I see that the once humble fly reel has now been elevated to equal status with the fly rod, with prices to match (insane in my view); that saltwater fly fishing is exploding in popularity (good! spread everyone out!); that videos have shoved aside books (reading being an endangered activity); that fly-fishing luggage has become a serious status item (no one fishes at home anymore; the trout are always two thousand miles away); that the commercialization and deification of Norman Maclean proceeds apace a decade after his death (enough already!); that it's getting harder to find flies with barbless hooks (bring them back, please); that women are being looked upon as the new frontier by the merchandisers (designer waders, special rods, vests with tampon pockets: male condescension at work here, or sensible adaptations?); and that whoever is writing catalog copy should in the name of truth and decency be hung.

A healthy corrective to all this and a far more interesting pastime is going back to look at fishing catalogs from an earlier era. Beside me as I write is something I've saved for thirty years: a catalog from Norm Thompson Inc. in Oregon back in the days when the company still sold fishing tackle.

A couple of things are at work here. First is the price of bamboo rods (pre-graphite days these), which sets my mouth watering with retrospective greed. A Winston eight-footer with two tips comes in at an even $100; an Orvis seven-footer at $67.50 (postpaid!). New fly lines are $11; a Hardy *silk* line is $19; a Hardy LRH reel, $27 (extra spools for $10). It only gets better as the pages go on. An assortment of dries tied by the famous Art Flick is $4.50 for ten; Muddlers tied by Don Gapen, their *inventor,* are 65¢ each. The catalog is printed with a kind of modest, understated dignity; it includes, among other interesting pieces of advice, an excellent article on casting by the late great Jon Tarantino.

A golden age, surely, but in truth the prices were just as out of reach for me as a teenager as today's are out of reach for me as an adult. I did manage to save $39 for a Hardy fiberglass rod, which has served me well ever since, but I don't remember ever having enough for anything else.

Nowadays what I mostly order from catalogs are flies, since, as mentioned, I'm no tyer. This year I notice, scanning back over my list, that I've pretty well abandoned standard mayfly imitations altogether, except in their parachute versions, the rest of my dries trending toward caddis patterns, midges, and attractors. For nymphs, I favor Pheasant Tails, weighted mostly, a few with bead heads, most without. In streamers, Woolly Buggers have pretty much replaced traditional patterns for me, except for the Golden Demon (death on brookies up here) and the Muddler. The chief oddity on my list are wet flies; I'm one of the last to fish them with any frequency, and I have to scrounge around some before finding catalogs that stock them.

When I added up this year's total it came to $253—a little too much, what with my daughter needing braces, my son wanting to go to soccer camp, various bills becoming due. I went back to the drawing board, crossed out ruthlessly. This time, I told myself, I would scrape it down to a bare-bones essential list, no vagaries, no experiments, no gambles, just the working everyday flies I absolutely needed. . . . Did so, added them back up, came to a grand total of $346.68.

4. DO LUNCH.

Talking about trout fishing has always been a substitute for the actual act; some people are more adept at the former, some are good at both. I enjoy it under two circumstances: trading battle stories with old friends who share many memories; and talking with complete strangers, seeing how quickly we can find common ground in rivers, landscapes, and fish.

It's a large and complex subject, conversational fishing, but here I'll say only this: how endearingly eager so many of my friends are to launch right into their latest fish stories, to the point where even the usual conversational staples—how's the family? how goes work?—are skipped entirely. One of my friends, having returned from fishing in Argentina, called me up the other night with a full report, in the course of which it became clear that he had been home only seconds—that his very first act when the taxi dropped him off wasn't playing with the kids or checking in with his wife, but calling a buddy with all the glorious details.

So, come March, I'm more than ready to go out to lunch with anyone who calls, knowing full well what the agenda will be, willing to do my share of listening, expecting some patience in return. There's a lot of planning and scheming that goes on during these lunches. I've noticed the deeper in winter the date is, the wilder and crazier are our schemes (*We'll fish in Bosnia, take advantage of those brown trout streams no one's fished in years*), and that the closer to spring we get, the slightly more realistic they become

(*Hey, rainbows feed on walleye eggs, right? We tie up some egg imitations, head right down to Kenny Dam, and—bingo!*).

But lunches can booby-trap you, too. Last week a friend who never steers me wrong called with an interesting proposition. He was sponsoring a Russian fishing guide who was in this country for a monthlong internship at a tackle shop, the better to learn about the business end of fly fishing and acquire lessons he could apply to his budding capitalistic enterprise back on the salmon rivers of the Kola peninsula.

Would I have lunch with him? my friend wanted to know. He wouldn't be able to stay more than a minute himself, but he was certain the two of us would hit it off.

All my fishing lunches are at the same venue: a large, friendly Chinese restaurant one town south of here. Two minutes after sitting down, my friend arrived with Andrey. He was a stocky man with a drooping mustache, dressed in a leisure suit of black denim. With a smile that was more of a grimace, he shook my hand—with his *left* hand, his right being stuck, like Napoleon's, at a right angle into his jacket.

My friend grabbed a wonton and left, leaving Andrey and me alone.

"Have you enjoyed your stay here, Andrey?"

He scowled. "Of course," he mumbled, with great sarcasm.

Whoops.

"Uh, it's a shame you're not here during the trout season. I could have taken you out."

He shrugged. "On my river, we have salmon of fifteen pounds. The small ones."

Whoops again. Time to order, try to get communication back on track . . . but we never did. For some reason, he and I started out on different wavelengths and never managed to find a common one. For him, this was one blind date that was obviously a bore, the only redeeming factor being the Chinese food or, better yet, the Chinese service, which amazed him with its attentiveness; he kept glancing at his water glass, amazed to find it was forever filled.

I did my best to carry the conversation along—English wasn't the problem, since he spoke it perfectly—then we pretty much gave up and ate in silence. The situation was saved by the lucky intervention of my pal Tom C., who happened to come in and did somewhat better with Andrey than I had. We finally managed to learn something of Russian fly fishing; we were interested to hear that, according to Andrey, the same scoundrels who ruled things under the Communists now ruled things under democracy, and that the chances of his getting a fishing lodge established on his river without paying massive bribes was slim. Which explained his gloominess, I suppose.

After what seemed like hours, the waiter brought our check and the fortune cookies. We had to explain to Andrey what they were.

"My future, yes?" he said with the first real animation he had displayed. Breaking the cookie apart he read his, read it twice, then, with a snort of disgust, crumpled it up and threw it at the lo mein.

5. BUY A LICENSE.

We usually get a big snowstorm the first week of March, and often we'll get a second hard upon this, but by the last third of the month winter seems to have broken its back. The robins return for good, ditto the bluebirds; the sap is running, not only in trees, but in human beings, so it's hard not to feel the anticipatory exhilaration of spring.

You'd have to be made of granite not to give in to this. The new lightness in the air seems to require an appropriate tribute, and one of mine is to stop off at our local country store, plunk my twenty dollars down for a fishing license.

"Early this year, aren't you?" Tammy says, rustling behind the counter for the proper form.

I shrug. "Figure I'd nudge spring along."

Tammy, speaking of spring, is very obviously pregnant, happy with it, excited, but a bit on edge as well. Since I'm the first one to buy a license this year, she has some trouble with the new form, and what's worse, there's suddenly a long line of customers, the phone is ringing, and there's no one else to help.

"You want the cold-water species license?" she asks distractedly, searching the form for the right box to check off.

"Yep."

"Hunting, too?"

"Just fishing."

"Shellfishing?"

We both laugh.

Finishing, she pushes it across the counter for my signature, then hands it back with the little booklet listing the rules and regulations—and there, Wetherell is official once again.

"When's the big day?" I ask, tucking it in my wallet.

She smiles at her stomach—a bit ruefully. "Tomorrow!"

Buying a license up here, while I fully support it, is something of a formality, since with the fish and game budget being so strapped, warders at a premium, I'm never checked. Thus, a month later, wading into the cold shallows of a favorite brook trout pond, I was more than a little amazed to see a green-jacketed warden emerge from the puckerbrush behind me. "Gotcha!" his expression seemed to say—or maybe it was just the quick flash of guilt that comes over you in these situations, innocent or not.

"How's the fishing?" he asked. Then, a second later, "Can I see your license?"

I thought he looked at it with more than usual concentration, glancing up now and then to compare description and reality. Hmmmn. Red hair? Yep. One hundred and ninety pounds? Yep. Six foot three? Yep. That left only one thing.

"There aren't any clams in this pond," he said. "Lobster neither."

Say what?

"Here," he said, pointing to the upper corner of my license. "You've got yourself a shellfish license, mister." He hesitated. "And I *bet* you have a story to go with it."

6. ANSWER LETTERS.

One of the best fringe benefits of writing about fishing is that you get lots of mail from people telling you how much your book meant, far more letters than you receive when you publish a novel. Fly fishers tend to be literate folk, so enthusiastic about their passion their letters all but bubble over, and of course there's that ancient and venerable swapping instinct at work as well; since I've told a story or two of my own, it's only fitting that I share theirs.

Fair enough, especially since receiving such letters is one of the real highs March brings (and for whatever reason, late winter is when most of the mail comes in). I always answer each one. I'm pleasantly surprised by how many turn out to be from people who don't fish at all, readers whose letters begin *"Dear Mr. Wetherell, I've never fished in my life, but something made me pick up your book and I just want to tell you how much it meant."*

This is not to pat myself on the back, but to try and understand exactly who my readers are. That books are one of the oldest, most successful collaborations in the world—a collaboration between writer *and* reader—is perhaps so obvious it doesn't need mentioning, but it's a blind collaboration, between people who in most cases never set eyes on each other, their only meeting ground being those words.

The people who respond best to the ones I'm responsible for seem to be those who, in loving the natural world, rivers, lakes, and ponds, respond passionately to a note of celebration played even as wobbly and discordantly as mine. Dogmatic, know-it-all fly fishermen, pompous technocrats, the macho boys or jet-setters: I never get letters from these, and I suspect if they read me it's with a mix of bewilderment, incomprehension, and anger . . . but now I am bragging, wearing their disapproval like a badge.

Give me readers of simple hearts and subtle minds! Readers who know what a river feels like full on the chest! Readers who see in trout the richness of the living world, and find in books something of the same wonder!

But here, let me quote from a handwritten letter I received just this week; see for yourself what I'm talking about.

> *Dear Mr. Wetherell,*
>
> *My name is John Grienan. I'm 61 yrs. of age. And recently retired from my Sales job w/a Tool Co. after 32 years.*
>
> *I have owned a camp on Sheckle Pond in Vermont for close to 27 yrs. My Wife of 38 yrs. & I purchased this Piece of Heaven when my 2 Sons were Young & Still at Home. Outside of my Wife, 2 Sons & 5 grandChildren it's my most precious possession.*
>
> *Your book is the first & only book I ever read. I'm not proud of that but it is a fact none the Less. I read Magazines, Short Stories & the paper cover to cover, but till your book I never finished a Book.*

> *Mr. Wetherell I'm writing to you to tell you how you put on paper all that I thought & felt while walking my river. I've sat like you on the Bank & dreamed of someday putting into words all the feelings I have about my River, but you have said it all & I guess I needn't put mine on paper. I'll just Read & Talk about yours.*
>
> *If you ever want to Try my River, please contact me. I would be proud to Guide you through & maybe even catch a few Browns, Rainbows or Brookies to Boot & Introduce you to some of the wonderful People I have met on my river.*
>
> *Thank you.*
>
> *p.s. Please forward to Mr. Wetherell.*

That's a collaborator for you, my partner already, the two of us putting our backs to the words and together wrenching out some meaning, then some more, than still more, until finally we've built something where the words disappear—a riverine world in which we dwell simultaneously, if only for the space of a page. Thank you, Mr. Wetherell? No, it's thank *you*, Mr. Grienan, for a high so unexpected and delightful it has brightened what is otherwise a cold dreary day here, lumined my spirits with it, so I feel like a man should feel heading into spring—alive and giddy, silly with sap, madcap, coltish, corny, ready to foxtrot, jitterbug, levitate, *soar*.

Hey, I'm a fishing writer! Drop me a line!

7. WRITE A BOOK.

What's important to remember about fishing stopgaps is that none of them work, not entirely, not for very long. Substitute fishing is substitute fishing; its pleasures, though real enough, are like solitary notes waiting for a melody to sweep them along. What they're up against is not just the frustration of waiting for that oh-so-distant opening day, but the lingering regret from the season having ended the year before—for me, a real downer that colors my mood well into winter. Here for a six-month cycle fishing and all the joys that come with it has been woven into my everyday life, and then suddenly—just because the northern half of the planet happens to be tilting on its axis away from the sun—it *isn't,* and the bittersweet emotion attendant upon this is not easily assuaged by anything but another year immersed in the same cycle.

And the weather doesn't help. That first spell of warmth never lasts in these hills, nor does the second, and the storms seem to get fiercer and more perverse the further beat into spring. Worse, each fair interval is more beautiful than the last, until anyone who is at all sensitive to fluctuations of the vernal mood feels like they're being embraced by a skillful and experienced lover (there is no other analogy) who knows how to tease and stroke until you're all but crying from desire . . . and yet the climax never seems to come, so the stroking, pleasant as it is, loses its point.

Spring, when it does arrive, with its chorus of bird calls, its high-pitched choir of peepers, the warmth that not only pours down from above but wells up from below, seems so new and overwhelming it demands an extravagant response. For my children, it's going outside with a kite, or kicking through last year's leaves in search of balls and Frisbees abandoned there in the fall; for our retriever, it's kicking up her heels like a puppy, chasing her tail; for my wife, it's digging in the top inches of soil, the miraculous inches, so warm, so particulate, so suggestive of bursting life. Kissing a pretty girl, driving with the top down, knocking out fungoes, painting the birdhouse, caulking a boat. Spring is response time, always the response.

Writers, too, even those most thickly ensconced behind impervious study walls, are asked for a springtime response. Often, this can take the form of starting a book. For this writer (for whom study walls tend to be more like drafty, permeable membranes), it can sometimes take the form of writing a book on fishing, a journey which—having made it twice before, seen what I wanted to see, shown my slides, written my postcards, paid my entry fees, left my tips, gotten home healthier, less wealthy, more wise—I never thought I would embark on again.

My determination to *not* write about fishing became, in the seven years I stuck with it, something like the ice that covers the Connecticut River near my home. Glacier-like, solid, seemingly immune to change, caring not a whit for the variations in warmth and light that create such longing in humans, it appears in March like something that will literally be there forever, having forgotten how to be anything but what it is: *ice*. And yet, even in the deepest recess of winter, there are other forces, less spectacular, less obvious, and by themselves less powerful, that work invisibly to erode and chip at it from all directions, until, between one day and the next, the ice is gone, and anyone staring at the blue, sparkling water where it had been could only with the greatest difficulty be able to imagine there ever having been ice there in the first place.

As in ice, so in writers, and the only thing left to do here is explain as best I can those little nudgings and chippings that have once again caused things to flow.

The first of these is that my fishing days have gotten into the habit of coalescing themselves around stories, and it's a tendency I enjoy and approve of, to the point where I'm not sure I could call a halt to it even if I wanted to. Yes, I enjoy fly fishing, but I also enjoy thinking about myself fly fishing, and it's just this added bit of refinement that gets my stories started. Or put it another way. I've a habit of noting things on rivers I wouldn't notice if I wasn't interested in getting them down on paper, sharing them, and I find that if I throttle this urge, I see less, notice less, enjoy less, even *catch* less . . . and so the selfish and unselfish motives are pretty well mixed.

And as a close corollary to the above, I feel I'm not quite done with sharing my adventures with my collaborators, feel their own interest quite strongly, and—again like that ice—find I'm not proof to it, not by a long shot. It's not just those letters, the pleasure they bring, but the fact that I sense my readers so clearly, me who hardly ever meets any of them face to face. In writing novels, I've always found the dreaded creative isolation to be a real and painful fact, one that has to be struggled with constantly, and yet I feel none of that strain in writing about rivers and the natural world, and I'm just human enough to find this comforting.

And more experience is waiting on line, demanding to be described so as to come fully to life. This is another motive and a strong one. Trips to western rivers; new friends made fishing; watching my children learn to fish; a new river I've fallen head over heels in love with or, rather, a new portion of a river I've known for years. Runoff, current, sunshine . . . the ice starts to crack.

And there's another nudge, a strictly personal one this time. Having written two books on fly fishing, I want to write a third partly because of the magic that resides in the number three. Troika, trio, triad, trilogy, trinity, *trico*. The first book on the left, exuberant and rambling, an unabashed love letter to my favorite stream; the second in the middle, more realistic and sober, an examination of the fishing motive and why it takes hold; the third here on the right, impelled by a reformer's zeal this time, the feeling that the tremendous surge in popularity that fly fishing has undergone in the last ten years has seen much lost in terms of quietude and contentment, modesty and simplicity, solidarity and fellowship, and since these are the qualities at the very heart of my own love for fly fishing, I want to do what I can to preserve them, sing their virtues. A desire, that is, to steer fly fishing back to its roots, when Izaak Walton, in all tranquillity and fullness of heart, could describe fishing as "a rest to the mind, a cheerer of spirits, a diverter of sadness, a calmer of unquiet thoughts, a moderator of passions, a procurer of contentedness that begats habits of peace and patience in those that profess'd and practis'd it."

Thus, my intentions. What kind of book will it actually turn out to be? I honestly don't know, not at this stage, not when the long season of commitment a book represents hasn't properly started yet, other than these preliminary jottings, this slushy March of good intentions. *Humble* is the operative word here. Someone starting out to fish the Battenkill or the Madison would hardly say, "I'm going to catch three rainbows sixteen inches long, then top things off with a brace of twenty-inch browns"—not a fisherman I would care to know, at any rate. No, what he or she would say is, "I'll be fishing the river tonight, and my hopes are high, but it's a funny game, fishing, so you never know, though at a minimum I bet I'll catch a delightful helping of earth, water, and sky."

It's the attitude that motivates this book—to find words fit to match the beauty of the locales it inhabits. I want it to be a random, artless kind of book, not one that is shaped too deliberately; I want to give the writing a chance to wind (as fishing writers of an earlier age might phrase it) hither and yon, pooling up eddies when it needs to, forming broad slow oxbows that double back on themselves, sluicing off the rocks into wild, chaotic chutes, carving its way through a willing landscape of collaborative hearts.

21

This may involve being a cheerleader at times, celebrating the joys of rivers, lakes, bays, and ponds just for the sake of celebration; there will be other times when this is not possible, and the cheerleader in me will give way to the Cassandra, the Jeremiah. This is the writer's double role now, since here at the millennium it's impossible to write honestly about nature without confronting many hard things. Yes, a trout is the most beautiful example of sentient life I know, so perfect in its adaptation, so colorful, so strong, that merely to see one finning in the shallows, taking a mayfly with that delicate rise, tip, and fall is enough to anchor an entire book on; this same trout, scientists warn us, can contain enough poison in its tissue that a person concerned about their health should eat no more than two or three a year. No, celebration alone is impossible, but only the worst pessimist would be blind to the beauty of the natural world that still surrounds us, though we try so hard to spoil it, tame it, beat it back.

In angling terms, this book will stick to the middle ground. I'm neither expert nor duffer, but someone who is lucky enough to have made fishing a part of their everyday life. Hence, there will be many detours into other subjects, other ground; my best fishing days are often those where fishing barely fits, and I see no reason to change this pattern when it comes to writing about fishing.

So be it! Here is the source—my hands on this keyboard, this head full of memories, this surge of happy intention—and there out this window are the granite hills and limestone meadows down which all this will run. Where the current will cut deepest, whither it will lead, no man, least of all this one, can know.

And one more thing before starting, the answer to the question I didn't quite solve at the chapter's start. When exactly is that border when the fishing season in imagination becomes the fishing season in fact? In the quirky, stubborn state I live in you're allowed to fish beginning January first, but this, in a personal-responsibility kind of way, only throws the decision back onto the individual, makes the answer an impressionistic one, having little to do with the calendar and everything to do with mood and feel.

I can't give a precise opening day, but I can give a precise opening moment. Taking a break from writing around ten when the sun warms my study window, I wander out into our meadow where one last snow drift rises like a humpbacked island from the sea of flattened grass. Down the side of this island runs a rivulet of water, cutting a small bluish channel through the wood-flecked snow, fanning out when it touches earth, thinning to transparency, then collecting itself again, running down the all but imperceptible declination formed by our hill. I've watched this before, but now, straddling it, staring down, blinking in the sunny brightness, with a sudden intuitive knowing that must match an animal's or bird's, I realize there is no refreezing in store for this drift, no more storms waiting to add to its bulk, nothing in this landscape but a myriad of such trickles running down the hills in perpendicular interminglings, restoring to full and vibrant motion the brooks they fall into, the streams, the rivers, the life in the rivers, the life in whoever loves that life— and that it's the wide and exhilarating sense of these contained in the trickle at my feet that, for this fly fisher at any rate, starts the season once again.

Times Seven

IT WAS A GOOD DAY, not a great one. Only three trout, but one each of the species we catch here, and so victory enough to commemorate in some appropriately small way. On the inside of our kitchen door, hung high for convenient jotting, is a calendar—the family kind, with pictures of grazing holsteins and date squares so fat and open they seem to generate appointments on their own. On impulse, I took out a green marker from the drawer near the stove and printed my own message in what little space remained on May 20 between *Dentist appointment 9:00* and *Return IRS call late p.m.*

Three trout. Sugar River. Brook, Brown, Rainbow.

On impulse—and yet more than that, too. It was my way of saying "Take that!" to the messages already scribbled like a maze across the month, giving them the metaphorical finger—the appointments to have the brakes checked, the boring lunch dates, the nagging reminders to do this and that. The following day, managing to sneak out for an hour before breakfast, I crammed in another entry beneath those already written across May 21.

Two smallmouth Clarkson Pond.

This was surprising in a way, because I've never been one to keep a fishing journal. Every few years I receive one for Christmas, beautifully bound, often gorgeously illustrated, with lines for recording stream, species, fly, water temperature, and hatches—even space at the bottom for what is referred to in the more expensive editions as *Musings.* Each year I resolve to start making entries in these, but always wimp out at the last moment; there's something too business-like and precise about it, a note that is only exacerbated when friends who do keep fishing diaries tell me how valuable they are in forming a "data base."

No thanks. But the quick, harmless jottings on the family calendar—these soon become my regular habit, the brief formality of taking out a pen, finding the proper date, squeezing my little triumph in what space remained, becoming—like a beer from the fridge—part of the ceremonial withdrawal from fishing to nonfishing.

Any habit needs limits and bounds. Mine is that only game-fish can be listed, which here in northern New England means the three trouts, largemouth and smallmouth bass, landlocked salmon, and pike. When circumstances warrant I may add the size and appropriate punctuation to the entry, as on July 15: *One brown 22 inches Connecticut River!* Once, teased and toyed with by a big northern for a good twenty minutes, only to lose him at the net, I felt justified in listing *½ pike!* There's only one more rule—any size counts, so a two-inch trout goes on the calendar beside the large one, all fish, within species, being equal.

I can sense purists objecting already—numbers and fishing do *not* go along. There's a danger of turning our pastime, like so much else in this culture, into a matter of keeping score. Those big squares on my calendar. What do they resemble if not the inning squares of an old-fashioned baseball scoreboard, the kind that once in fond memory rose above the bleachers at Ebbets Field? But, to my credit, I've resisted the temptation to think of it in those terms, count every fish as another run. No, the pleasure for me is in marking and acknowledging the seasonal rhythm of a fishing year—the two or three trout wrested from a grudging April, the sudden surge in numbers during late May, the June so crowded with entries I begin to write sideways along the calendar's edge. And reassurance is there, too. No brookies yet from Franklin Pond? Well here, rummage through my bookcase until I find last year's calendar, flip quickly to May and discover I didn't catch my first one until the 15th, the year before on the 17th, so nothing to worry about, right on schedule.

Beside me on the desk is the calendar from the season just completed. It was an excellent year. I managed to get out often, the weather was cooperative, and by playing some lucky hunches I was able to find fish all the way through the first week of November. At the end of each month I added things up. June was the leader with 97 fish; August, with family trips, the slow spot with only 13. Totaling up each month in turn, I find I caught and released a grand total of 356 fish.

Now, this is a modest enough figure—roughly a fish for every day of the year, which, considering how many of those days are actually fishless, seems a most appropriate figure to shoot for. It's the total of someone who goes out two or three times a week two or three hours at a time. Certainly, on the right water, fishing hard, you could match this figure in three or four days of good fishing, and there are anglers who do just that. But it occurs to me that my total, so definite and final on the calendar where I inked it in, is of and by itself a completely misleading number, one that doesn't begin to convey the complexity and richness of a fishing year. For starters, it represents only gamefish: bass, trout, and pike. If I were to count *every* fish landed—the pugnacious bluegills that swerve about like flying saucers, the rock bass that punch so hard before collapsing, the gregarious perch and misanthropic pickerel, the chubs that rise so annoyingly to a fly— I would have to double the total, which in one swift calculation brings me from 356 fish caught per year to a more realistic 712.

But stay with me a bit further here. Even this figure isn't the end of it, and if we're talking not of fish beached or netted, but fish I was somehow *involved* with, the number grows even higher. What about all those fish that rose and I missed? The deep strikes that never resulted in a hookup? These were part of the experience, too, often the most exciting part. In midsummer, fishing in desultory fashion on a slow-moving river near my home, I made a just-for-the-hell-of-it cast toward the center in featureless water over fifty feet deep. Instantly, as if the fish had been waiting there for just that very thing, the water burst apart, the uplift so violent the popper came spitting back at my face, causing *me* to duck so violently the canoe nearly overturned.

Nothing. The pull with no bottom to it; the grasp that comes up empty.

A big fish certainly, but what? An adventurous bass roaming far from shore? A stray salmon on his lonely, homesick way back to the Ammonoosuc? One of those mysterious trout that are rumored to live in the river, slow and weedy as it is? The fish we miss are the ones whose shades we remember longest, and there are hundreds of them each year, surely at least three for each fish actually landed, which—going back to my original 356—adds another 1,068 to our total, bringing it up now to 1,780 fish I was busy with last year, in one way or the other.

And what about those fish we manage to hook, but lose on the fight? There was a big, heartbreaking one on the Upper Connecticut last autumn—a monstrous rainbow that took a Royal Wulff five yards from where I was casting, stayed attached for the first jump, but snapped the tippet on the second as I stumbled frantically to get downstream. Even a modest computation would include at least one fish escaped for every one landed, another 356, swelling the year's total to 2,136 fish.

The iceberg is emerging past the tip now, with more yet to come. What about all those fish seen in the shallows that despite all our efforts refuse to strike? I'm not particularly adept at spotting fish in a river, even with Polaroids, finding my myopia no match for the complex shadows on the bottom, all of which I'm more than willing to believe are trout, but even so, there are dozens I *do* see in the course of a year, managing inevitably to scatter them apart on my first reckless cast. Bass, too—there are days after a high-pressure system moves through when they roam the shallows with their jaws set in a puckered and painful way, as if they had locks through their jaws, locks no key of mine can possibly turn. How many of these fish are there each season, seen but not caught? Let's keep it on the conservative side, a quarter of my 356, which still swells the larger figure to 2,225.

I fish with my family a lot. Anyone who has young children knows how strenuous an operation this can be. Child Number One's rig readied, bobber adjusted, worm attached, the whole to be tossed gently sidearm to a likely looking spot. Repeat operation with Child Number Two's outfit, only the process is interrupted by Child Number One's bobber disappearing . . . frantic instructions to reel in, landing the perch for her, rebaiting the hook, casting it gently out again . . . back to Child Number Two, who meanwhile is near tears from impatience; get his outfit rigged now, but before it can be cast Child Number One has managed to get her hook caught on some weeds, go over to free her, then back to Child Number Two, who really is crying this time . . . soothe him, cast his rig out, keep watch on both bobbers simultaneously . . . rebait, recast, detach perch, apply sunscreen, rebait, recast, feed, and water. . . . In comparison, wading upstream on the Madison near Slide Inn seems easy, an effortless stroll.

I have to be tactful here, and a loose accounting is in effect, but let's say Dad has a *hand* in catching just about every fish. That's easily another 100 fish a year, and a new subtotal of 2,325.

Had enough? What about partners I go fishing with, all the fish I net, or even the battles where I merely sit and cheer them on? I have a friend who took two rainbows over 25 inches from the Bechler River in Yellowstone last year, fishing hoppers in a wind hard enough to knock us down, and watching him play those fish on a 6X tippet from the bank, intent as a heron, balanced right on the border between panic and calm but balanced there perfectly, was one of the high points of the season. Fish with the right person, someone who shares the excitement with you, and the fish soon become joint property; stories told subsequently are apt to begin, "Remember that first rainbow we caught on the Bechler?," that expansion in pronoun, *I* to *we,* being the identifying mark of a real fishing partnership. Certainly there are 150 of these *mutual* fish a year, enough to bring us up to 2,475.

And maybe this is where we should let the figure rest, though there is another category that would at least double the figure, perhaps even triple it. We see the fish landed, of course, even many of the ones that get away, but what about that surely larger class, the unseen fish that spot our lures, follow them for a second, but then turn away in boredom or contempt? There must be hundreds of these a year. Occasionally you'll see some sign . . . a brief swirl well back of the fly; a shadow deep beneath your streamer as it's withdrawn from the water for the next cast . . . but for the most part they remain invisible, the great fishy majority of the unconvinced.

But let them go. Two thousand four hundred and seventy-five fish landed, lost, spotted, felt, or shared is still a huge number to be in any way involved with, and yet a much more accurate representation of the fishing year than my original and too modest 356. A season turns out to be not grudging and niggardly, but full of fish, fish won and lost, opportunities squandered, near misses, vicarious success—fish everywhere, fish by the thousands, fish galore! Any diarist, any calendar jotter like myself, should keep these in mind, even if choosing to commemorate the few in honor of the many. I picture them there right now, the trout and bass recorded in those calendars from 1990 and 1991 and 1992, squeezed in what space remains beside the exhortations to *Pay mortgage!* or *Change shocks!*, reducing these forgotten and burdensome chores to their proper insignificance, feeding on the quotidian like it was a new and tasty form of crustacea, until the decades go by, the calendars yellow, and all that remains in the record of those years is water and fish and those generous moments stolen from the trivial when against all odds we manage to connect.

May 29

IT WASN'T MY KIND OF FISHING, which is why I said yes. *My* kind of fishing had been consistently lousy; with the rivers so high, the ponds so cold, I hadn't caught anything longer than a salamander all month. So yes, by the time my friend Ray Chapin called with his unexpected invite, fishing for shad immediately below a nuclear power plant in the middle of a mob under a broiling May sun seemed the very thing.

Words can attract you even more powerfully than fish, and this was the determining factor. *Shad.* That's a word worth saying out loud, with its sibilant start so suggestive of speed and stealth; its hard, rakish *ad* sound, rhyming with *bad* and *cad*; its quick, compact finish, suggesting a fish that packs a considerable punch. Free-associate with all the fine old American connotations . . . *shadbush, shad roe, shad bake, shadfly, shadberry, shadrach* . . . and you have something that exerts a pretty strong fascination, even though, at the moment Ray called, I had never seen one in the flesh.

Neither one of us had the slightest idea how to catch one either, but what the hell. We hitched Ray's boat trailer to the back of his car, stopped at Wings for some meatball subs, drove an hour south to the big dam that crosses the Connecticut just below the nuke, kicked the winch loose, shoved the boat in, hopped aboard. The shad run, exterminated by the early dams, has pretty well been re-established, and now substantial numbers of fish are finding their way ever further north.

Were we in time to hit the run at its height? For once in my life I was hoping for a crowd, not only as evidence that the shad were there, but to steal some hints as how to catch them. The dam forms a huge pool here, the cement of the spillway merging into bankside cliffs that are even higher. In the middle of the current a flashy runabout was anchored, monofilament lines stretched taut out the back like thinner versions of the power lines that crisscrossed overhead; around and behind it, zipping in and out from the dam's base, was a smaller aluminum skiff with a big antenna mounted in the middle, a man sitting in the stern with earphones, squinting in concentration; closer, on the rocks, were (not to put too fine a point on it) a shirtless redneck bully and his entourage of Budweiser-swilling friends. With the pylons, the cooling towers of the nuke, the nearby traffic, all this seemed perversely appropriate. Put a couple of effete fly-fishing sissies in the middle and *voilà* —the scene was complete.

"What do we do now?" I asked. Caught in a whirlpool, our boat was spinning around out of control—but it takes more than this to break Ray's concentration.

"We put on one of these," he said, tossing me something that, compared with trout flies, seems lurid in its redness. "Shad dart. I tied some up last night."

You're supposed to fish these slow and deep, something we didn't know at the time, so we fished them fast and shallow, since, as mentioned, the very notion of *shad* seems to demand speed and haste. Over on the Vermont side of the river was the fishway, and we could see a family peering over the fence, staring down and pointing, so it seemed pretty clear that there were indeed shad passing within reach of our darts, probably shad in great numbers, and yet two hours went by and we had nothing to show for it but sunburn.

There was a saltwater kind of feel to this fishing, what with our long casts, the expanse of the river, the anchored boats—even the sunbathers on what passed for a sandy beach. The longer we went without catching a shad, the greater my respect for them became. Shad are so powerfully anadromous that even the presence of them in the general vicinity carries the flavor of salt air, far horizons, wheeling gulls. Standing in the bow of the runabout, trying to keep my balance, hauling away, furiously stripping, I felt stretched, mentally and physically both, and it felt good to be so.

When it came time for lunch we put-putted downstream until we found a sandy island shaded by some huge silver maples. Up by the dam all was commotion and hurry, the river industrial, but a few hundred yards away a much more quiet, pastoral mood was in effect, and both of us were pleasantly surprised by how lush and rich the landscape was on both sides of the river. Three states come together here, but they all seem invisible; there you are down on the water hardly aware of anything but the steep and sandy banks, the swallows darting out from them, the trees silhouetted obliquely against the sky, a glimpse now and then of wide, darkly furrowed fields, the rush of current against the boat's bottom.

Exploring, we thought we might stumble into some fish, and we did—but not shad. Tying on a chartreuse Sneaky Pete, I tossed it out to where a sandbar cut abruptly down into the current, and immediately found a nice three-pound smallmouth. They were stacked up there in line, strong, gutsy river fish, just waiting for our poppers; as I've noticed before, they always seem to hit these, not from hunger, but from an outraged, betrayed kind of anger, as if the poppers didn't represent food at all, but little totems or miniature gods the bass had once worshiped, but then had been disappointed by in some essential way (allowing the invention of bass boats?), to the point where the fish struck back at them every chance they got.

Which, of course, is a lot to read into a bass hitting a popper, but how else to explain that ferocious explosion? I've been searching for the perfect analogy to describe it for many years now, and—since I love smallmouth so passionately—perhaps always shall.

Once the sun got lower we went back up to the dam to take another crack at the shad, though by now the day had the feel of going fishless (at least with shad), and that's a pretty hard notion to shake.

Then a funny incident happened (and yes, it also had the feel of being a funny-incident type of day). A pontoon boat festooned with fishing rods steamed into view from downriver, heading right for the center of our little flotilla. There was a suntanned man steering—in age and demeanor he looked like someone who had retired too early and was having trouble filling up his days. In the bow stood his attractive, suntanned wife, ready with the heavy anchor. Reaching us, he had her heave it . . . but apparently it wasn't the right spot for him, because not two minutes later he shouted for her to pull the anchor back up. A second spot they tried, closer to the dam in the heavy current, but this wasn't quite to his liking either, because no sooner had the boat come taut on the anchor line than he had her pull it up again, hand over straining hand.

This went on at least six times—which was obviously one time too many. Suddenly the wife turned her head, said something we couldn't hear, something especially pungent and to the point, and the next thing we knew the pontoon boat was disappearing downriver the way it had come. We looked at the fishermen in the boat next to us; they looked at us—we all burst out laughing.

Yeah, that kind of easy, relaxed day. Holding each other's gunwales, we talked for a while with the man in the antenna boat, discovered he was doing research on the salmon smolt released upstream, seeing how many made it through the dam intact, then, on our way in, drifted over closer to the Budweiser boys, and found them to be pussycats, all excited about the shad they had caught the day before. Pulling the boat out, breaking down our fly rods, we took our own beer out of the cooler and strolled over to the concrete fish ladder to see what we could see.

There were shad all right, hundreds of them, three or four pounds each, as compact and purposeful as their name suggests. That each one of these had sailed right past our shad darts without interest seemed beside the point now; it was wonderful just to watch them, admire the way they turned, turned a second time, then shot over the next step on their way up and across the dam. Their color, a silvery brown that veered toward yellow, seemed peculiarly foreign and exotic, emphasizing their migratory quality, as if they were indeed emissaries from a watery kingdom far more colorful than the one we knew.

"Incredible," Ray said, pointing at the biggest. "Beautiful, huh? Wonder what they feel like on the end of a line?"

I shrugged—but at the same time felt those little sensor muscles in the middle of my forearm, that higher, vital fishing pulse, go taut in sympathetic vibration as I imagined their power

. . . the power to run three hundred miles up a once polluted river and gladden us on a perfect May afternoon.

PART TWO

The New River

The New River (1)

IT WASN'T LOVE AT FIRST SIGHT or second or even third. Seen early in June, its water still busy with springtime cleansing, the river has the gray-silver color of a playground slide—a dangerous, slippery one, with treacherous steps and no handrails, something a prudent mother wouldn't let her child on alone. And while a river that has the potential to kill you is in many respects more interesting than a river that doesn't, on this perfect late spring morning, as I pulled on my waders, looked around at the radiant bowl of mountains, meadow, and field, smelled the mica sharpness of rushing water, sensed that vernal crescendo of bursting and triumphant life, I was even more strongly than usual in no mood to drown.

So *gently* was the operative word. To the river, this silver-colored, unknown thing racing past the alders twenty feet below, I would bring gentleness, stealth, efficiency, calm—this though my skin had already tightened in anticipation of its temperature, my heart was thumping in anticipation of its force. Anyone with a sense of prudence, anyone approaching the down slope of life, will always be respectfully frightened of a strange and powerful river; it's perhaps a tribute to the fact I wasn't quite over the hill yet that this fear, though real enough, only contributed to the fun.

Booted, wadered, armed with the lance of my fly rod, the visor-like brim of my fishing hat pulled low against the midday sun, I clanked toward the banks ready for battle—and then, remembering the prudent part, found a boulder and sat down to look things over. I had picked the most obvious spot to start: a dirt pull-off where the river first came into sight from the road. Of course this was the spot most likely to be fished most often, but this sometimes can mean it's the spot most deserving of fishing often—and in any case, this is exactly the kind of self-serving logic you start playing around with on a river where otherwise you don't have the slightest clue.

What I was looking at as I sat there shaping up my nerve was a river twenty yards in breadth, with a current fast enough to form haystacks against the granite boulders that forced it into a curve. On the far side, the New Hampshire side, was a cornfield that had just been planted; in the middle distance I could see the red tractor, the sunburned farmer, moving at the head of a vertical halo of chocolate brown dust. Higher, looking up, were the northern peaks of the White Mountains—pyramids, a child's perfect drawing, and yet jumbled, lying in a plane that seemed remote from the one the river ran through, pictures hung on a separate wall. The Vermont bank, the one I sat on, was steeper, with enough alder and raspberry vines to make getting into the river a challenge. A bit to my right—the water that had drawn my immediate interest when I parked—the current pushed hard into the bank to form a long sluice flecked with bubbles, running between a corridor of smaller, sun-bleached boulders, their tips white with bird droppings and the dried skeletons of bugs. There were no insects showing, but the air had the humid softness that generates mayflies. And, while this is a hard concept for the non-fisherman to grasp, over everything—sky, fields, boulders, even mountains—hung the distinct and unmistakable aura of trout.

And it was all new to me—that's the important part. I was badly in need of a new river. The one I've fished religiously for ten good years had declined to the point where I could no longer pretend the poor fishing was due to seasonal fluctuations—fool myself, that is, that it would someday bring me the rewards and pleasures it had in its prime. Too many houses had gone up too close to its banks; too many lawns had received too much fertilizer; too many trees had been felled; too much shade had been hacked away by the highway crews; too many gravel pits were now gouged into the hillsides, too many trout decorated too many stringers—too much of the kind of abuse and neglect whose effects are malicious, downright criminal. Its native trout had disappeared completely, and even the stocked ones were gone by July, so what had been a living, thriving miracle was now nondescript and empty, anystream U.S.A.

But that wasn't all. Even when the fishing was still good I found myself getting bored with its challenges; they came to resemble pieces of a dearly loved puzzle, assembled and assembled again, but always in the same pattern, so its solving became too static, simple and flat. The rainbows in the Aquarium pool were suckers for a Royal Wulff twitched across the current, but that was just the problem—they were suckers for it, time and time again. The longer we fish for trout, the more we want them to come to us from behind strong defenses—and the more we realize that those rivers where the defensive is strongest form, in trout fishing terms, the major leagues. This new river at my feet was most definitely the major leagues, perhaps the only river in New England that could be mentioned in the same breath as the rivers out West. To take the analogy a bit further, it's what I was feeling as I sat there tying on a fly—like a rookie stepping up for his first at bat in the Fenway Park of his dreams.

And even that, when it came to motives, wasn't all that was at work. For many years I had ridden the boyish bubble of sheer animal exuberance that can last well into a man's thirties—and long past this as well, but only if we actively work at it, seek out new challenges, ones that are taken seriously, but not grimly so, our motives trending toward, at least in this one area, the care and nurturing of pure delight. Many fishermen change wives at this point in their lives; me, I was ready to fall head over heels for a gorgeous new river, a trophy river, one I could grow old with in perfect content.

Strictly speaking, this wasn't a new river at all. If I waded across here, set out downstream along the eastern bank, in less than a hundred miles I would come to my home, set on a gentle slope above the river and facing past a farm. The water there was deeper and slow, thick with smallmouth, pike, and walleye, but no trout, other than the occasionally stray monster that stumbled down from one of the tributaries. A hundred miles is a sizeable gap in a river; that the bright rushing water here had some connection to the lazy river downstream would have been hard to accept, other than for the strong circumstantial evidence of their having the same name. And yet there were other threads, now that I looked. Here the banks were steep and sandy, the resort of swallows, just like at home; silver maples leaned out over the shallows, just like at home; like at home, honeysuckle blossomed wild right down to the water. The farmland, what I could see of it, seemed every bit as rich and fertile as it did further downstream, the river's gift to an otherwise flinty land.

And yet it was a trout stream here, not much more than a good cast wide, something I could wade across if I picked my spot, get to know with my feet, thighs, and chest—a river that

came in flashes and swirls rather than a broad, seamless pushing; not a silent film, but a river with a sound track. The transparency was different, too. At home the river was opaque,
mysterious; here it was clear and mysterious—mysterious in the
way of a mirror, hiding as much as it reflects. I edged my way into
the current behind the shelter of the first large boulder, felt for
the first time the water on my legs; felt a cold chilling power that
even the neoprene of my waders did little to stop; felt that prod-
ding downstream nudge on the back of my knees; found I could
withstand it; found, half to my amazement, that this river, like
other rivers, would accept my intrusion after all.

Again, *gentle* was the key word. One of the things that
occurred to me as I waded my way out was that slip in the wrong
place, hit my head on a rock, and the river would give me a fast
ride home. Working out my line with fussy little shakings, coming at last to a comfortable stance on firm gravel, pivoting,
stretching, I tossed a Muddler toward the gray-white seam
where the bubbles swept past the rocks . . .

And immediately caught a fat fourteen-inch brown trout.

Well no—but that's the way the paragraph is supposed to
end. It is impossible for anyone possessed of the genetic minimum of hope necessary to be a fisherman to step into a new river
without expecting a fish on their first cast. Since this so rarely
happens, it's best to get the little bump of disappointment over
with early; I stripped in fast, loaded up my fly rod, sent the Muddler back to resume searching, fantasy stage over, ready now to
deal with the bright, flashing reality spreading out past my legs.

Fun reality—I'd forgotten how much fun. Right from those
first exploratory casts I was caught up in what for an experienced
fly fisher is probably the purest delight of fishing a new stream:
applying those generalities experience has taught us elsewhere
to an entirely new set of specific conditions. In general, current

surging against a bank, channeling itself into a deep run, is a prime spot for trout, offering shelter, shade, and a reliable conveyor belt of drifting food. The experienced fisherman sees this at once, makes for it, hardly gives it any thought. So too with pools—our eye seeks them out, finds them even in what, to the casual observer, appears hardly more than a vague slackening in a current that seems uniform. Of course, each river has exceptions, spots that don't conform to these patterns at all, or do so in quirky variations that aren't at first apparent; one of the interesting things about fishing a new river is learning not only how the general rules hold, but how they don't. But, in lieu of specific tips, the a priori rules and patterns come first, giving a comprehensible frame within which to find the intensely specific. It is why, if luck stays neutral, the experienced fly fisher can catch trout faster than someone who doesn't have those miles of wading, probing, questing under his or her belt.

Reading the water is one of the few talents in my very small arsenal. Partly because I've been doing this for nearly forty years, partly from intuition, I seem to be able to sense where fish are holding, though, of course, catching these is an entirely different matter. In theory, the spot I'd picked out to start was a good one; in reality, the current was far too fast, sweeping my streamer along before it had a chance to sink to the trout's level of interest. And I was fishing downstream with a steep bank on my right—for a right-handed caster, a tough, uncomfortable position. Across the river was an inside curve where the river was slower, but to get there I'd have to tiptoe from sunken boulder to sunken boulder, in water well over my head; in other words, though with a lower water level it would definitely be worth trying, I was fishing something of a dead end. So okay, I was learning. Chalk it up to experience, file for future reference, and, cutting my losses, climb back out onto the bank, pull my waders down, finish off the blueberry muffin left over from breakfast, drive further upstream.

This random in-and-out probing is one of the ways you get to know a new river; you have to pay your dues with lots of wrong hunches, air balls, sheer and maddening dead ends. As I drove along I kept one eye on the river, trying to determine where to try next. From the highway the water had that intimidating silver color that had so impressed me earlier, so I still felt wary of trying just anywhere. But in trout-holding terms, it looked more seducing the further away the road curved, and this made it even harder to pick out a spot than if it had all looked barren.

But this is no way to scout out a river, no way to drive. After about a mile I spotted what I'd been looking for all morning, put on my directional signal, turned onto another sandy pull-off, this one leading right down to the river through a cut in the bank, as if there had once been a crossing here for wagons or carts.

It was a fly fisherman who had caught my attention—the first one I'd seen. He was barging through the alders toward his pickup, his waders dripping in wetness like the fur of a sleek young moose. Not so many years ago the profile of your typical fly fisher was bulky and endearingly plump, what with those crammed-in fly vests, those baggy waders that never quite fit. This has changed in the last decade, thanks to neoprene, designer vests, Gore-Tex, and pile; this fisherman was taut in the contemporary, fascist style in sportswear, everything a uniform, everything a statement. You can picture this type of fly fisher not only getting dressed before a mirror, but saluting when he's done.

So I should have known. Right from the start I should have known. But being the fool I am, I rolled down my window, came out with that time-honored opening line. "Any luck?"

The fly fisher—he looked to be in his thirties—grimaced and mumbled something I couldn't hear.

"I saw some caddis down below," I said. "Anything showing?"

A real scowl this time. He continued past my window to the pickup, threw his rod in, backed up with a squeal of brakes, drove off.

Screw you, buddy—I didn't have to be clairvoyant to read his thoughts. It's the prevailing attitude of too many fly fishers you meet on the stream these days, their competitive fires fully stoked, every fisherman looked upon as an intruder, so you find yourself facing not a companion in a gentle, carefree sport, not a fellow pilgrim, but a competitor, naked and brutal and in-your-face.

I'm not that old, and yet I can remember a time when this was different. *Any luck? Well yeah, not too bad, a nice fifteen-incher and lost something bigger besides. Midges, small gray fellows. Here, you might put this on if you get a chance. Tied it myself last night. How about you? Nice river, huh? You know it well? Let me suggest a place you might want to try a little further upstream.*

Fantasy? No, since it's happened to me often, and once upon a time led to some of my best moments on the water. Sure, fishermen have always been secretive, but they once were secretive with panache, and an encounter like this would have been ornamented by some imaginative fibbing, all of which would have been part of the game, perfectly understood on my part, returned in good measure, a decoration of the essential good advice we both swapped.

Not anymore. Rule that out as a means of getting to know a new river: asking another fly fisher for advice. Luckily, I had another card up my sleeve, and I decided to play it now, my one real bona fide tip, given me by a friend from the old school when he heard I was heading north.

"There's that old grass landing strip up past Lemington. Army used it for emergencies during the war, and the town still keeps it cleared, God knows why. Anywhere along there is good. Nymph water mostly. Fish down from the windsock and watch out for that bull."

You can't miss it, he added, and naturally I should have understood that to mean the place was hidden in vines, invisible from the road, impossible to locate short of chartering a plane. After many wrong turns into pull-offs that petered out in mud or rocks, a bumpy driveway leading to a landlocked farm, I finally stumbled onto the obscure landing strip and its ancient windsock. This last was fastened to a corroded hoop mounted on a rusty iron pole; the windsock itself, condom shaped, was full of holes, so in the light breeze it could only manage to flop forlornly, not stream out erect. Between this the *temps perdu* atmosphere the landing strip cast off (I thought of Spitfires, vintage planes), I had a good feeling about the place even before I climbed down the bank.

As it turned out, my friend had steered me to as prime looking a fishing spot as any I'd seen in a very long time. Here a river that was forty yards wide narrowed to a uniform twenty-five, deepening with that concentration, going from just barely wadable ten yards out to well over my head in midstream. This deepening ate up the current—the surface moved in the kind of even, controlled pace that is perfect for a drifting fly.

The approach was made easy by a long sheltering island on the Vermont side; it was no trick at all to cross the narrow channel that led out to this, then, using the island as my combination base camp, observation spot, and lunchroom, fish upstream or down. Over on the New Hampshire side, perched there like a watchtower deliberately erected to spy into the pool's center, was a small summer cabin, a man outside cutting wood. Upstream was Vermont's tall Mount Monadnock, tilting the horizon into a greenish slant. Downstream, backed by the twin Percy Peaks, was more of that wonderful riverine farmland, shaggy with unbaled hay that, judging by the smell that wafted upstream, had just been cut. Though I looked carefully in all directions, there was no sign of any bull.

What struck me right from the first moment was the combination of power and intimacy contained in this stretch; here was a river that had thirty miles behind it and four hundred left to run, compressed into a channel I could almost cast across, and yet it was quiet, easy, in no hurry whatsoever, easily wadable over a perfect gravel bottom—a place possessing that trouty atmosphere even more intensely than the first spot I tried, so I knew that I would *have* to catch a fish here, and probably a good one.

I waded out to where the current was strongest, pumped my rod up and down like a drum major leading off a parade, then dropped a weighted stonefly at the bottom of the scrappy cliff on which sat the little cabin. The current bellied the line downstream, slowly straightened it, and then, just when I decided *nothing*, pulled much harder and faster than the current could have managed on its own. A trout, a fine trout, but what occurred to me right from that first instant was how sharp and compelling that first strike was, out of all proportion to the trout's eventual weight—that what was really taking hold in that instant was the new river itself, its promise, its beauty, the joys it would soon bring; that if it's not correct to speak of W. D. Wetherell falling in love with the Upper Connecticut River at first sight, it's eminently fitting to speak of his falling in love at first tug.

Indulge me for a moment while I write into that tug everything I can. For while half of me, the part that resides in hands, arms, muscles, and eyes, was busy keeping just the right amount of pressure on what was turning out to be a thick-bodied, headstrong rainbow, the other half was listening to the kind of voice we never hear except in retrospect, and then hear so clearly we can't believe we didn't actually hear it at the time. *Enjoy this, fella* was what the voice was saying, in a baritone so musical and strong it could have been the river's. You're going to catch lots more fish here over the years, this is only the first, so concentrate, enjoy it, savor it right from the start. You're going to make friends with the man who owns that cabin, though you'll never exchange words—a pantomime kind of friendship, where he'll spread his arms apart and shrug a question mark when you first wade into the pool, point down emphatically when he spots a good fish, clasp his hands over his head like a prizefighter if you catch it, shrug his shoulders and frown if you scare it back under the bank. You'll fish here often with your fishing partners, rotate through the pool with them, have fish on simultaneously, call out to each other those little telegraph messages of advice, disappointment, victory, interrogation. Here in a few weeks you'll be up to your neck in hatching caddis, the pool alive with trout, so their rises spread into one another and you can arrange your drift to cover three fish at once. You'll camp here this fall, know what it's like to tumble out of the tent into the cold damp fog of morning, see it with a whistling sound be pierced by a squadron of mergansers racing upstream, the fog in tatters on their backs. You're going to find this pool, this river, an excellent antidote to the staleness that creeps into a forty-something life even in the best of life's circumstances—an aphrodisiac of fishing that makes you discover new delights in a sport you were almost beginning to lose interest in. You're going to sit on that sandy dip in the middle of the island, find it a perfect backrest, pour yourself countless mugs from your thermos of tea as you sit there watching your friends fish, or the trout rise, or the play of sunlight off the water when it's too hot to do anything else. You're going to forget to be careful going down the muddy bank and slide in like an otter, not once but a dozen times, get your waders soaked, shiver in autumn snowstorms, catch fish almost every time you come here, and take it in stride when you don't. Enjoy fella, throw your strength against that fish, push your belly into the current, overwrite all you want. *Enjoy fella, because life can be ironic and bitter and cruel, and it's only moments and places like these that redeem it, so watching carefully, putting your heart into it, for God's sake get it right.*

Which, of course, is a lot of portent for one trout to carry. He was up to it and then some; after that first long run, he came slanting back toward me, still stubborn, still likely any second to run—and there, that's exactly what he did, leaping clear of the water just when I decided he wouldn't jump at all. Holding my rod high, stepping carefully over a bottom with contours my boots weren't used to, I found a comfortable stance at the head of the island and brought him in. A good fish, the kind with shoulders, the color oddly pale on its flanks (the pink washed out into a watery silver), but more than made up for it by a dark shield of reddish-maroon over his gills—a color that made me think, when I first saw him flashing, that it was a brook trout, not a rainbow at all.

A wild fish, too—there was no mistaking that kind of robust good health. I put my thumb on his jaw, widened my fingers along his flanks, then, pivoting on my pinky, extended my thumb again. A span and a half, or nearly fifteen inches.

Soon I would learn that this was the kind of fish you were looking for on the Connecticut. There were bigger trout (state-record size, ten and eleven pounds), but for the most part this was the quarry that made the trip worthwhile—strong, wild fish with just enough heft that you couldn't take them for granted, boss them around. I've noticed this before, how critical the inch is that separates the almost good fish from the really good. A thirteen-inch trout is a decent fish in this day and age, but give him just one more inch, add on the corresponding depth and maturity that starts to kick in at that length, and you're talking about a *serious* fish, one that seems, though composed of familiar elements, an entirely different compound, with four times the explosive punch.

Releasing him, I waded back out into the pool and worked my way downstream, throwing that black stonefly out toward New Hampshire, then letting it swing in the current back toward Vermont. There were three more good fish within the overlap of a dozen casts. Toward the tail of the pool, where the water thinned and quickened, the fish were smaller, brook trout, small wild browns. On my last cast, just before heading back to the island for some R & R, something hit the nymph even harder than that first rainbow, so hard that when, missing him, I stripped the line back in, I found the hook had broken at its bend.

In its way, this first fish lost was as symbolic as the first one landed, suggesting that my future with the river would include many disappointments to go along with its many pleasures. Making the long drive north only to find the river the color of a chocolate milkshake from a thunderstorm during the night. Seasons of drought when the trout, the best ones, turned belly up and died. Days when fish were everywhere, and yet I fished badly, making them flee in aesthetic horror. Good fish gone on the strike, leaving me with that desperate feeling of loss that makes up in intensity what it lacks in duration—the feeling that if you hadn't been so quick or so slow or so stupid, not only the fish but happiness itself would have been landed, redeeming everything that happened to be wrong with your life at the time in question. Yes, it was good to have this reminder early, find it to be a real river, not one flowing in dreams.

It was late enough now that the Vermont side was deep in blue shadows from the bankside pines. I continued downstream through the edge of the rapids, then down through another series of riffles and pools, knowing it was a long walk back to the car, but keeping on anyway, even though I was no longer fishing. I'd found what was obviously an excellent stretch of river, caught enough trout that my first day was a success, and now I wanted to top things off with a last bit of reconnaissance, start linking the scattered stretches of river I had seen so far into a comprehensible chain.

One aspect about this portion of the Connecticut immediately enchanted me. Over the years the current has cut deep through the surrounding clay and loam, so, wading, you can be a good twenty feet below the level of the surrounding countryside, making it feel like you're fishing in secret within a self-contained groove of water, rock, and sky. There on the banks are vines and creepers, great clumps of hay the tractors can't reach, trees in the muddy spots, the raspberries and sumac that help hold things together. By June these are already high enough to add to the tunnel effect, their leading tendrils curving out toward the river so the banks are doubled. Still higher, above the vegetation, above the willows, the sky seems channeled in the same narrow blueness, so the entire world, not just the river, is rolled into that flowing north-south line. Occasionally, one bank will crumble away of its own weight, giving you a glimpse over farmland toward mountains, but for the most part the outer world remains invisible, except for the smell of hay, the rumble of tractors, a distant chainsaw, the harmless rush of invisible cars. More than anything, this serene, self-contained effect is what causes the bittersweet feeling I have when climbing back out at the end of the day; it's a narrow strip of paradise you've been wading through, but paradise all the same.

Time to go? Not quite. Up in the sky the light was still yellow enough to pass as afternoon, but down on the river the shadows had already joined from both banks, so what I waded through was the last V of sunlight left on the water, my waders separating this into a smaller, darker arrowhead that stayed in close to my waist. With dusk, in that perfect June stillness, mayflies were hatching and caddis, too, enough that I had to blink as they brushed against my eyes. I'd been wading along gravel all the way down from the landing strip, but here near an enormous silver maple, in what I would learn was one of the river's characteristic tricks, the bottom suddenly turned to mud, the water deepened, and I had a difficult time scrambling back to the bank.

But no matter. I had spent the whole day trying to read the river by various clues, portents, indications, trendings, and now between one moment and the next, in the fullness of that hatch, the river was revealing itself to me for free. Trout were rising everywhere in the water I had immediately judged fishless— good, deep-bodied sips, the kind that make it seem like it's not invisibly small flies the trout are sucking down, but the river itself, saucer-sized sections they take away as trophies, cast in bronze, stash who knows where. *Voilà*—they could have been shouting this out loud. One over by the sloppy beaver lodge; another dead center ahead of me; still another under that leaning, fungus-scarred birch.

It's one of the most splendid things about trout, this rising to feed visibly out in the open; the effect is what you would experience in Vegas if the blackjack cards, as you watched them in despair, ready to give up, started giving quick little flips so you could see their faces. *Here we are, come and catch us;* as graceful as these rises are, you can't help but imagine them being made without a certain nah nah nah-nah-nah tone that can drive you mad.

This tone was uncalled for, at least tonight. I wasn't going to fish for them at all, but sit there watching on the bank, absorbing the day's late lessons. The fish were unreachable anyway, not without a float tube or canoe. So, put that down on the list of resolutions that had been growing longer all afternoon. *Come back with canoe, evening, Sulphur Duns, Olive Caddis, long leaders, 6X, stealth.*

I needed my flashlight to get back to the car. As I stumbled through the brush, one of the briars managed to strip the flashlight away, but even in the dark the grassy runway was unmistakable; a half hour later I was back at the car, taking apart my rod, gulping down the dregs of tea still left in the thermos, and with it some aspirin for my overworked back. I could hear the river now—realized that as intensely as I'd been staring at it, I hadn't taken the time to adequately listen. It was a soft noise, surprising in a month when everything in nature has its voice turned up full blast, muted even further by all that meadow grass, so the effect was like silk being poured over velvet, poured in a tall pitcher, shaken on the rocks.

Back next week on Tuesday if I could finish work on time? Maybe spend the night, wake up early? It was good to think in those terms, good to feel the old kind of excitement kick in. I had done what I had to—given the river the chance to work on me— and it had made of it a thorough job, so if it wasn't love on that first intimidating sight, not love on that first chilling immersion, it was certainly love now—or how else to explain that intense and happy sorrow I took away with me home?

The New River (2)

SINCE THAT FIRST AFTERNOON on the Upper Connecticut, in the ten years since, I've been back well over a hundred times—a statistic that probably carries no significance for anyone but me, yet one I'm childishly pleased with as a mark of my devotion; it's as though I've entered upon a marriage so perfect I renew my vows every chance I get. And—why not admit this?— I'm head over heels in love with the river still, think about it often while I'm away, pine for it, dream about it, rave about its virtues to family and friends, soberly come to terms with its imperfections (which in any case are of a kind to make me love it all the more), take solace from the memory of past assignations even as I find excitement in plotting my next. When it comes to infatuation, the Connecticut and me, it's the heart's whole nine yards.

And it's remarkable, looking back on that first introductory season, how fast the routines started to form that have served me well in the years since, with little variation. The early-morning start, often in darkness, the stars bright out the window as I go around the kitchen on tiptoes trying to bag together a lunch. Tom driving up in his pickup right on schedule, or maybe Ray in his little Volkswagen—the quick stowing of rods, vest, and waders, the brief remarks about the weather, always putting a good face on it, at least at this stage, when even snowflakes on the windshield can be given a propitious slant. The drive up the interstate, high on its ridge overlooking the valley, the two of us talking over prospects, all but rubbing our hands together and chortling in anticipation of the swath we'll cut among these trout. The sunrise over the White Mountains to the east, the summits capped by lenticular clouds that multiply their dimensions in purple-gray swellings . . . The radio, the news, fading out in static, the last noisome whispers of the world we're leaving behind . . . Breakfast at our favorite truck stop, the eggs and home fries and homemade toast appearing so fast on our table it's as though the short-order chef has gotten word of our coming through CB radio, anticipated our order well in advance. . . . Leaving the interstate for slow, stately old Route 2, route of the logging truck, the school bus, the moose. The first view of the Connecticut near Lancaster, giving us a clue as to what kind of water level we'll be fishing in—the banks sandy here, the water slow, but a reliable guide all the same. On through Guildhall, the neat, compact little village where the road cuts north. The vexing question of whether to continue up the west, forgotten side of the river or cross over to busier New Hampshire for the added speed . . . Northumberland, Groveton, North Stratford. . . . Trout water at last, the river not slow, sleepy, and deep anymore, but fast, broken, and rushing, so even through the window glass, in the eight A.M. sunshine, it gives the effect of well-shaken champagne poured down a silver-bronze chute. Fishable? Yes! A bit high, but not too high, and transparently clear from bank to bank, the boulders on the bottom doubled by their own blue shadows. . . . The talk about where to start in, not abstract and hypothetical like it was two hours ago in the darkness, but urgent now, needing a fast decision. Trophy Hole? Perfect. Slug our way up to it while we have all our energy, fish it while the sun has the stoneflies rock and rolling up a storm, then the current on our backs for the long wade back. . . . Parking, unpacking, getting dressed—stopping now and then to blow on our hands, our breath in front of us in crystal balloons that pop apart on anything but the softest syllables. Socks on, waders on, vest on, rod strung up—the ritual that is so important a part of the fly fisher's start. . . . And then the river itself, stepping into it—hardly feeling anything at first, not even coolness, not until we're well out into the current and sense that old familiar pressure on the back of our waders, like a reassuring pat on the rump as the river welcomes us for the 101st time.

There are other rituals in the course of a fishing day, but it's the river that's setting the agenda now, with much more variation, so things never again become quite so formalized as they are when starting out. I've gotten to the point where I need every one of those steps along the way, feel, rightly or wrongly, that if one or two are left out then I won't be able to catch as many fish, or at least not quite as much enjoyment—that substituting apple jelly for marmalade at breakfast will result in botched casts, missed strikes, and overall futility. In life, ritual seems to work best in small things and big things, coffee breaks or weddings, and for me, fishing the river is a mix of both—and yet the small comes first, to the point where I think a fishing day could be described not in terms of fish landed, but solely by all those small, dearly loved familiarities woven into the fabric of a fishing life. The downward, not unpleasant tug a fishing vest gives on the shoulders when you first put it on; the sharp taste of split shot as you bite it closed; the gossamer shine of tippet material blowing in the wind; the fine, almost invisible spray of wetness that comes off a fly line as it shoots forward and drops. "All this is perfectly distinct to the observant eye," Thoreau wrote of delights just as small, "but could easily pass unnoticed by most."

With all this by way of introduction, starting now on the second stage of my exploration, it's time to come forward with what is simultaneously the most extreme and yet sincere bias in my entire arsenal of fishing beliefs: that the most important factor in fly fishing for trout is not casting ability or streamcraft or entomology, but coming to appreciate and understand something of the landscape, terrain, history, and culture of the region through which your river flows.

This is heresy of course—suggesting that anyone setting out to fish the Henry's Fork might do better to bone up on local history than consult guidebooks to the various pools; that sitting in bars and diners listening to the locals talk weather, politics, or crop prices ultimately might be more useful than hiring a guide; that time spent loafing beside a river looking out at the distant views is in many respects even more valuable than time spent studying the water. All this not only flies counter to prevailing wisdom, but hardly makes up a corner of it at all—and yet I'm absolutely convinced it's true.

Why? Remember, we're talking bias here, personal hunch and intuition, and it would be hard to isolate the direct causative factors between understanding the region and understanding the fish. Certainly, to try to come to an appreciation of the larger scape a river runs through demands of a person a certain investment of time and attention—and it's exactly the ones who are willing to do this who are most likely to bring the same qualities to their fishing. Then, too, it slows a fly fisher down, looking outward like this, and in fishing, slowing down is half the battle. Too often we come to the river caught up in the fast, frantic pace of the artificial world we're seeking to escape, and this man-made schedule is the first and most onerous burden we must shed. A river can't be rushed—this is the first rule of fishing, the second, and the third—and so any time spent along its banks *not* fishing is a worthy investment, slowing, quite literally, the speeding hands of our inner, overwound clocks.

Listening to the locals, trying to learn who they are, what their lives are like, pays off, too, since these are the people you will encounter along the stream, and there is simply no talking to them unless you're willing to make some effort to share their world. Fly fishing is more art than science (though fully neither), and one of the criteria for being good at it is the ability to take into simultaneous consideration many varied threads. Local knowledge is one of the most important of these elements—and how else to tap it except by meeting it halfway?

I could back up my theoretical arguments with a more prag-matic one, point out that the best fly fishers I know happen to be the ones who have an instinct toward the elusive "feel" of the region they fish in. I could also point out examples of fly fishers for whom none of this counts—those who are too wrapped up in their own passion to focus on anything but the fish there in front of them. Not understanding the country's rhythms, they're locked into the rhythm they bring from home, so there's a clash right from the start; not catching very much understanding, they will not catch very many trout. Not catching many trout, they will hire a guide next time, or buy yet another book on fishing how-to, and, because they are mistaken in their basic assump-tions, the river will always run away from them and never be grasped.

This kind of larger understanding and empathy is even more important when the region through which the river flows is an unusual, even quirky one, not at all what it first appears. The Connecticut River, starting as a small beaver pond only a few yards from the Canadian line, flows through a series of four mountain lakes of increasing diameter before spilling through Murphy Dam and becoming a full-fledged trout river in the town of Pittsburg, New Hampshire. Little bigger than a good cast across, fast, weed-slick, and rapid, it's not until it reaches Stewartstown and works the west out from its southwest trending that it becomes prime fishing water; from here on in, for the next 235 miles, it forms the border between Vermont and New Hampshire, though in a compromise that goes back to the former state's admission to the union in 1791, New Hampshire law still governs the river itself. Between Pittsburg and the vicinity of Lancaster the valley remains in the same overall pattern and can be spoken of as one; this is the region, the hard, gritty, difficult region, that in the course of my fishing trips I gradually began to know.

There's no shorthand name for this land, or rather, there are two names, both of which testify to the fact that it's a world apart. The Vermont side of the river, not without some irony, is called "the Northeast Kingdom"—a broad upland of granite hills and boreal forest, with a sparse, hard-working population settled in a few, well-scattered villages. Across the river in New Hampshire it's called "the North Country"—a similar landscape, only with higher, steeper mountains and, if anything, even poorer, more nondescript towns. The river valley proper, the broad floodplain, manages to seem as pastoral and gentle as anything further south (the white farmhouses, the old ones, are the most prosperous looking, best-kept buildings in sight and have been for two hundred years); a mile from the river on either side it's a different story. Here the upland begins, and it gives a rougher, grittier kind of feel, both in the landscape and in the habitation. Trailers covered in plastic; log cabins that are never quite finished and look horribly out of place; suburban-style ranch houses built from kits; sagging tourist cabins long since gone bust. This is as far from the familiar Currier & Ives stereotype of New England as it's possible to be, and much closer in feel to Appalachia, or timber country out West. Many of the towns, even in summer, manage to give off the worn, tired feel of perpetual November; Colebrook, the market town in the region's center, has the wide main street and slapdash, unfinished feel of a small town in Wyoming, though its origins date back two centuries. Like the river, the money has always flowed south here and probably always will.

An intimidating land, in the end—a region everyone agrees is "different," though without any of them quite agreeing where exactly the difference lies. Some would point to the terrain, those mountains that aren't as high as the Whites or as approachable as the Greens, but humpbacked and shaggy, less visited, more remote. Others might point out that, geographically speaking, this is very much a dead end—all the roads seem to end at border crossings which, for lack of traffic, always seem to be closed. There's the prominent French influence, or rather the Quebecois; the convenience stores have names like DeBannville's, the tackle shops Ducrets, and the churches are more apt to be cement, workaday Catholic ones than the stately Congregational churches associated with townscapes further south. Others, the wiseacres, might have fun with the moose, point out that moose-watching is the favorite (some would say the only) after-dinner activity. Sensitive observers, those who like to gauge a region in the faces of its inhabitants, might point to the people you see in diners or waiting by their trucks as they fill up with gas—their beaten mien and shabby clothes, the hill-country strength that stays hidden from strangers, yet you know must be there.

The difference is as much good as it is bad—people who linger here, make the attempt to know the region intimately, agree on this, too. There's the Connecticut, of course, its winding beauty, the locus for all that is soft and easy in the landscape, at least in summer. The beaver ponds lost in the ridges near the Quebec line, the brook trout lost and lonely in their centers, splashing to a fly like drowning swimmers to a life ring. Those moose that are everywhere—the wildness that clings to them like a second, more exotic pelt. The sense the surrounding forest gives of true northing—of boreal spareness and boreal flint, hills scraped as clean of ornament as the people who by stubbornness or inertia make it their home. The fact that it's a yuppie-free zone and always will be—that even its lakes haven't been gentrified or tamed.

You can take the difference even deeper. Living in most parts of America is like living on an inclined plane or gigantic slide, one that's tipped in only one direction, toward the great American middle ground—middle in jobs, middle in culture, middle in aspirations—so all you can hope for, growing up in it, is to drop pinball-like into one of several inevitable and ready-made slots. Here in this forgotten corner, up high on the height of land where the watersheds begin slanting over toward the St. Lawrence, the sense is of sliding away from America altogether, lives running in a totally opposite direction. Those radio talk shows in French. The poverty so pervasive the Depression is remembered as a prosperous time. The legends of bootleggers, draft exiles, and smugglers. The roll call of hermits and loners and misfits who have fit in here and nowhere else. The old communes and forgotten marijuana fields rotting away deep in the woods. The cranky politics. Yes, in a nothing direction entirely.

Cranky politics? For anyone driving through the region this is most apparent in the local custom of planting your property every four years with an orchard of campaign signs, ones that, once staked, are only reluctantly removed, so, feeling in something of a time warp already, seeing those signs, you're apt to think Ford/Dole is still running against Carter/Mondale. The shabbier the house, the more likely it is these signs will be for Republicans, though many are hand-lettered and crude, warning the U.S. out of the U.N., or vowing fidelity to guns. This is your basic old-fashioned cranky New Hampshire reactionary right, the kind you might have thought had crept up here to Coos County to die, were it not for the fact it seems to be spreading. There's an anarchistic flavor to it all; you get the feeling, talking to them even casually, that what these people really hate is any government interference whatsoever, though in the same breath they're berating it, they complain about how the state government down in Concord (or Montpelier) hardly seems aware of their existence.

It's a strange, potent brew. Who should stumble into its middle a few years back but Newt Gingrich himself, at the height of his power and influence, up north to do a little moose spotting, his euphemism for testing the waters in the primary state for a possible presidential run. Followed by an entourage of doting reporters, he stopped beside the Androscoggin near Errol for a photo op, started chatting up a fly fisherman waist-deep in the river (I picture the stampede scaring away a nice trout the fisherman was just on the verge of catching), who looked up at him, the cameras, the tape recorders, and scowled.

"You're the meanest thing that ever happened in Washington," the fly fisherman said, making the most of his opportunity. "Jesus, if it was up to you and your cronies there wouldn't even be a river here. Go home now—*get*."

Newt seemed considerably taken back at this—and as history records, shortly thereafter decided *not* to run for president that year.

This independent streak goes back to the region's start. Upper Coos County was once an independent country of sorts, the Indian Stream Republic of the early 1830s, when a free-spirited assortment of settlers, crooks on the lam, and wildcat speculators took advantage of a border dispute with Canada to create an "independent" country with its own laws and courts—an independence that lasted until 1842, with the signing of the Webster-Ashburton Treaty between the United States and Britain, and the arrival of the first militia units from New Hampshire to enforce the new boundary.

The only thing left of all this, beside the independent streak mentioned, is a historic marker on Route 3 and a good, characteristic story—a story about how a reporter was sent north by a Boston newspaper to interview a local Vermont farmer, who, when the reporter informed him the boundary had been redrawn and he now lived in New Hampshire, scratched his chin whiskers for a moment, pondered on the implications, then trotted out in his best laconic drawl, "Well, young fella. Mighty glad to hear it. Couldn't have stood another one of those Vermont wintahs!"

There's tourism here, of an old-fashioned blue-collar sort—northern New Hampshire is one of the last refuges of your basic $28-a-night tourist cabin—but nowhere near the kind that overwhelms the White Mountains every summer. Over on the Vermont side of the river there's even less in the way of visitors, and it's possible to drive the roads in October at the height of foliage season and never see another out-of-state car. What the region does experience in the way of mass invasion comes in appropriately bizarre fashion; the biggest event of the year in Colebrook,

for instance, is the "Blessing of the Bikes" in May, when thousands of motorcyclists from all over New England drive their
machines past a Catholic shrine set in a little grotto off Route 3.
The shape of the two states accounts for a difference in the
tourist flow; when you drive north in Vermont, you're driving
toward the broad base of its inverted triangle, spreading everyone out; when you drive north in New Hampshire, you're driving
into the apex, so everyone becomes concentrated.

Logging is the main industry here and always has been. It's
an important part of the economy in the lower parts of both
states, but up here it's the only industry and so it's more visible,
with logging trucks as common as cars, tote roads going everywhere, scars on the mountainsides from recent cuts, and, in mill
towns like Groveton, mountains of sawdust and the sweet, heavy
smell of boiling pulp.

Skidders, forwarders, and whole-log "harvesters" have made
logging into a humdrum, brutally efficient business, though one
that still carries with it more than its share of danger. It has its
romance, too, or at least its history of romance. A hundred years
ago the Upper Connecticut was the starting point for the great
logging drives on the river (still the longest in world history),
wherein the timber cut from the surrounding hills was sledded
over the snow every winter, piled on the river's ice, then—with
the help of a great deal of manpower—floated on the springtime
head of water down to the mills in Massachusetts, three hundred miles to the south.

Log driving was one of those hard, miserably paid jobs that,
like cow punching and whaling, seems more glamorous in retrospect than it probably did at the time. Look closely at those old
photos of rivermen posing by their bateaux or waist-deep in a
river full of logs: along with the pride and cockiness, you see a
great deal of plain old bone-weary exhaustion. For logging was a

brutal way to make a buck, one requiring agility and great strength, accomplished by a mix of Yankee woodsmen, immigrant Finns, and itinerant Quebecois. Rising before dawn to spend fourteen hours up to their waists in forty-degree water, ordered about by dictatorial woods bosses, preyed upon by hustlers of every stripe—it's no wonder rivermen were famous for their brawls (caulked boots festooned with case-hardened spikes three-quarters of an inch long were their weapon of choice, the flying leap toward the face their favorite tactic); the not uncommon murder (Canaan, Vermont, once had a lawless, rock 'em-sock 'em reputation to rival Abilene's or Dodge's); the devil-may-care attitude that made them spend their money as fast as they took it in (brothels, even up here at the drive's start); their chilblains, lumbago, and TB.

There have been attempts over the years to put a sheen over all this, make of these men heroic Paul Bunyans, but it's never really caught on, not with the Connecticut River log drive, since if anything the real interest and awe comes from remembering it realistically, as a remarkable example of the partnership between man's cleverness and the sheer driving force of nature. This was before the internal combustion engine, before paved roads. The Connecticut was the highway south, and every April the river was crammed bank to bank with rough, potato-colored logs, poked at by quiet, deadly earnest men—the logs jamming frequently (including the infamous North Stratford jam of April 1914, when thirty-five million feet of wood piled up in one extended jam thirty feet high), getting blown up when these jams proved recalcitrant, the drive sweeping downriver and taking with it every spring its sacrificial quota of a dozen or more lives. The bodies, those who no one claimed, were buried in pork barrels by the side of the river—in some cases, the victim's spiked shoes were hung on a branch by way of tribute.

The men in charge of these drives were not chosen for their compassion or sensitivity. The most infamous was George Van Dyke, a notorious bastard who saw nothing wrong with paying the men starvation wages, then finding every opportunity to cheat them out of those. But fate had its ironic way with him in the end. As he was watching the finish of the drive down in Massachusetts from his chauffeured touring car, the brake slipped and down he went over the steep bank into the river, never to rise again—the river's final sacrifice, for after this, with the interruption of the Kaiser's war and the introduction of the first trucks, the Connecticut River drives were never again the same, though pulp wood continued to be driven in the upper reaches until 1948.

There remain few visible traces of those days. At Lyman Falls you can see what's left of an old wooden dam and sluice; detouring into the woods to get to better fishing positions, you'll sometimes stumble upon the rusty old cables that held boomed logs in place . . . but that's about it. At least once during my fishing day I find myself wondering what the river looked like full of logs (and what it did to the trout—did they just hunker down until all the confusion swept past?), but it's a tough feat for imagination to pull off. Partly this is due to the fact that my fishing is in the clement months, so the river seems too relaxed and gentle to have ever been involved with anything so chaotic; partly because, on this side of the mythic enlargement time brings, the river now seems far too small.

But there are other moments when I can picture the log drives perfectly—autumn days, for instance, when the water is high and the leaves are gone from the trees, when the water seems darker, more furious, capable of something mighty, waiting only its chance. You can also sense something of the atmosphere of log-drive days just by cruising the roads, looking at the hardscrabble towns, sensing the feeling that something essential about the region, its very heart, has long ago been swept downstream.

The kind of man who found the log drives his escape—you can picture him, too. Earlier this season, after fishing just above the covered bridge at Columbia, climbing back up to my car, I discovered my keys were missing. I gave myself the usual frantic shakedown, then, thinking I had left them locked in the car, started prying at the window trying to get my hand far enough in to pull up the lock.

I had just found them (in the most obvious spot, naturally—the toes of my waders) when a pickup pulled over and a young man in a T-shirt and jeans jumped out, ready and eager to help. He was no more than nineteen, short and wiry, with a large French nose, bright blue eyes, and a restless, blinking kind of expression that couldn't stay fixed in one mood for long.

"Stupid of me," I said, holding up the keys. "Thought we were going to have to smash that window."

The young man grinned. "Why I stopped! Wouldn't have been the first time I smashed one."

I pointed to the chainsaw and gasoline cans in the back of his truck. "Looks like you're pretty busy in the woods."

"Nope. Not anymore. Got laid off"—he glanced down at his watch—"two hours ago."

"Christ. Sorry."

He grinned even wider. "No problem. They'll hire me back if I want. Old man Toller, he lays off everyone after nineteen weeks so we don't get enough consecutive in for unemployment. Then he hires us back, starts it over." He looked toward the river, spat without any particular malice, added by way of afterthought, "He's a bastard. Anyway, it don't matter. This time Sunday I'm out of here."

I played a hunch. "Army?"

"Marines."

Well, there it was, the North Country's other industry, the export trade that works full-time in so many of the forgotten places of the world, the beautiful places—sending its children to places less beautiful, less forgotten, less hard. With time, if he serves enough years for a pension, perhaps he will come back again to hunt and fish out his retirement, be able to enjoy the land without having to wrest a living from it, fight that particular battle at such long odds.

But he was excited with the future the way any young person gets excited when it comes time to tell the place you grew up in to go to hell. He pointed to the river, bent his head over so he could peer under the first tree limbs upstream.

"Always wanted to try a fly rod, see if I can keep myself from strangling in all that line. But up there's where you want to be fishing. Base of that little island, current scrapes out a big hole. Go there at night sometime. That's my secret spot, and here I am handing it over free of charge." He shook his head, ruefully this time. "What good is it to me? Hell, you can have them all. Up there by the town hall—good spot, too. You go down to where you see those cows, there's a little sandbar that'll take you right out in the middle of the river like a causeway. Rest is mud, so that's the only way. Good spot for browns. You know the old gravel pit down by the airport?"

On and on he went—my brain raced to take all this down; I kept wishing I had a tape recorder—going over his favorite spots, all the stories that went with them, so it was as if this were another part of the burden he had to shed before he could be free of the place and leave. Light, wiry, tough already at nineteen—it was easy to picture him growing up by the river in the days of the great drives, begging each year to go, being reined in by his mother as long as possible, until finally comes the day— and off he goes with his stagged kersey pants cut short in riverman fashion, the black felt hat, the peavey or cant dog, the spiked boots . . . and with a last farewell glance or, more likely still, without any backward glance whatsoever, away he floats down that river, never to return.

If getting to know a region helps you to get to know the fishing, the converse is true as well—there are few better ways to get to know a region than spending your time fishing it. Out in all weathers through six months of the year; poking your nose into all kinds of unexpected venues as you seek out new water; spending long hours in what is often someone's backyard; relaxing on the bank near a road, watching the traffic stream past; helping yourself to wild raspberries; learning where the old apple trees are that still bear fruit, if only by snagging your backcast on their branches; having the local flotsam and jetsam drift past your waist (red Frisbees, a blue Styrofoam "noodle"—whatever water toy is currently the rage); sliding down the midden heaps that river banks often become, so the archaeological perspective comes into play; talking to the local fishermen, the occasional duck hunter, the kids who come down to the river to throw stones in the current or hunt crayfish; being involved in a common pursuit people enjoy asking you about; making friends in the diners where you break for coffee or the bars where you go to celebrate your success. After a while, all this adds up. This is even more true if you go about your fishing quietly and modestly, so you all but become a part of the riverscape yourself—a tree, a willow, albeit one with eyes and ears and understanding.

I've often thought a good book could come out of this—a collection of tales on the order of Ivan Turgenev's *Sportsman's Sketches,* changing the hunter into a fly fisher who in the course of his or her exploring learns much about the local people and their customs, their heartbreaks, and sadness, their losses and their loves (Coos County, New Hampshire, badly needs its own poet or novelist; Frost never got this far north, and all the fiction writers seem to be concentrated on the Vermont side of the river). Just last week, fishing the river in the course of a long June day, I came away with enough locales to fill the book's first half. I started fishing behind the county old folks home, a Gothic pile straight out of Dickens, where people in wheelchairs sunning themselves on the terrace waved as I waded past; a hundred yards downstream (the state liking to put all its institutional eggs in one convenient basket), I passed the county "farm" that serves as the reformatory—young men this time, too busy piling up hay to wave, hardly noticing as, right below them, I landed a good brown. A little later, driving upstream, I fished behind some abandoned factories, had my thoughts filled with a *temps perdu* kind of moodiness that made me think again of the region's boom-and-bust history. In late afternoon I was caught in a sudden hailstorm, took shelter in DeBannville's, where French mémeres in curlers shook their heads and clucked in sympathy as the ice melted down from my hair. At dusk, waiting for the sulphurs to get going, I ran into a ninety-two-year-old bait fisherman, pumped him shamelessly, not only for information about the fishing, but for his memories of the old days (these took a morbid turn; most of his stories were of young men and women who had drowned in the Connecticut and people he knew who had helped pull them out).

And, just for the record, it's the bait fishermen you want to talk to if you're interested in learning equally about the fish and the region. Too many fly fishers these days are too narrowly focused on their pursuit, too businesslike and competitive to spare much time for my random kind of sightseeing; then, too, fly fishers you see on the river are apt to be from elsewhere, without much in the way of local knowledge. Spin fishermen, many of them, are pretty much just out for the afternoon, and when it comes to learning about the river, few have paid the requisite dues. No, what you want is the classic worm-chucking old-timer (by old-timer I mean anyone between the ages of fourteen and a hundred who fishes alone and obsessively and ponders the implications of what they discover), though once upon a recent time, to fly fishers with illusions of purity, these were apt to be viewed as our enemy. Secretive when they're fishing, they're talkative when you catch them at ease, and, like the teenager leaving me his secrets or the old man with his tragic stories, they're invaluable sources of information on the river you're trying your damnedest to figure out.

The hatch I was waiting for has started now right on schedule—little sulphur duns whose color is halfway between the white of a Cahill and the yellow of a daffodil just past its prime. The pool I'm fishing is a slow, even one, where the current, running broken along the Vermont bank, slides to the east, widens and slows, creating a living-room–sized terrace (with boulders for armchairs) that is almost always dappled with feeding trout. Catchable trout—for a change I feel pretty certain of this, and thus take my time getting ready, giving me the opportunity to go back again to one of the points I made earlier.

It concerns the river being the one locus of beauty in an otherwise hard-pressed land. Fishing the tributary streams, hiking the woods, driving the back roads, spending much time in town, you get the feeling that there is indeed much in the way of beauty here in this northern wedge of land, and yet it seems to come at you through a gauze, a scrim, that all but makes you rub your eyes in bewilderment, trying to clear them so you can see things plain. It's partially a scrim of poverty: the sense you have, even today, of what brutalities can be inflicted upon a land where the growing season is six weeks too short; a recognition that *beauty* is not a word that can be tossed around lightly in this kind of world, not with the shortcuts, stopgaps, and scraping that is visible on every hand. And yet, go down to the river, spend your days in its pastoral corridor, and the scrim literally dissolves; words like *lush* or *lovely,* prissy absurdities when applied anywhere else in the north country, suddenly become fully applicable, so it makes you see not just the Connecticut, but the entire region with a gentler, more forgiving kind of appreciation.

Wading out toward those fish, tugging line down from my reel preparatory to casting, picking out my spot, I'm aware not only of the merging cobalt rings spread across the current by the trouts' inhalations, not only the yellow-blue surge of water where the lowering sun hits the river and thickens it, but the tall, seed-heavy meadow grass that begins on the bank, the bristly hedgerow of sumac, black cherry, and ash, the first sloping esker with its birch and white pine, the staircase of spruce-covered mountains that leads toward the coral-dark sky—Vega at the top of it, the high steady beacon of a midsummer's eve.

"What a land!" I say to myself, not for the first time. "What a river!" and I want to shout.

Ten minutes left of dusk in which to appreciate it all—just time enough to end on a personal note, expose to light what my mind kept chewing over when it should have been concentrating on those trout. It was about the boy I met earlier in the season, the logger who was bailing out for the Marines. I thought of him, and in a strange way that surprised me; I realized I envied him, and not just a little.

What's going on here? A dead-end job, telling the boss to shove it, going off to the tender mercies of boot camp—no, it wasn't envy of any of these. Envy instead of what he probably hated most in himself: of having this hard, bitter land as the place he grew up in, the region he will—for better or worse—compare every other with for the rest of his days. I suppose it's a mixed blessing—mixed for those who leave, just as it is for those who hunker down and stay. Live your whole life in such a landscape and between tears and exhaustion and familiarity, the beauty disappears; it's someone like me, neither local nor stranger, who, when it comes to appreciation, has the priceless vantage point of standing halfway in between.

In this respect—and here again I'm speaking most personally—almost anything would be better than being from the suburbs. When that boy searches his memory one day it will be of dark forests and impetuous rivers and snowstorms in October; when I search mine, it's of patios and split-levels and manicured front lawns, spiced with nothing more romantic than the occasional vacant lot. I think of Chekhov, born into a family of peasants, vowing to squeeze the serf from his soul drop by hateful drop—and remember as a young man vowing in much the same way that I would force everything suburban from my soul or die trying. Hence, I suppose, those long hours on the river in all kinds of weather, fishing long past the point of exhaustion, dreaming about the river when I'm away, coming back every chance I get. Much has changed in my life—and yet the cleansing still goes on.

And maybe all this helps explain the feeling that comes over me sometimes that this hard northern land, with the river as its mouthpiece, is speaking to me quite plainly and directly—that if I haven't succeeded in articulating its message here, it's my own fault, not the region's. Certainly, having this feeling . . . of embrace, of acceptance, of an odd and powerful kind of pity . . . is a good, reassuring sign that I'm that much closer to understanding the river, making it, in the vain way we speak of such things, mine. If stage one was that first specific reconnaissance, then stage two is this working toward a more general, wider appreciation . . . and this is what I flattered myself that I had now, as, a tall shadow in a forest of round ones, I climbed out of the current, reached the crest of the bank, then turned my head quickly back toward the river like a man trying to catch it unawares.

June 9

Just when you think you've seen it all is the time to start admitting you've seen nothing. This is as true with sporting atrocities as it is with cultural ones, though I'm not sure which to file the following under. Twenty-four hours after the event, I'm still fuming, and write this partly in the hopes it will prove therapeutic.

Perfect weather. June and gloriously so, temperature topping out at seventy, the water at a perfect fifty-five. Lilacs at their peak—bouquets line the road. Mayflies on our windshield so dense and yet so airy it's as if a special welcoming committee is draping my Toyota in a fine muslin sheet. Visions of plentitude, visions of grandeur. Thirty-fish day? Thirty epiphanies? Both feel in reach.

Then, the fall to earth. Our favorite spot, our secret spot, a gray Mercedes parked there in its insufferably squat, arrogant way. Empty rod cases in back. Silver nails in our golden hopes.

Ray and I make a good team. He's good at speechless indignation; I like to curse. "Fuck!"

(A quick calming reminder to myself from Father Walton: *"I would you were a brother of the Angle, for a companion that is cheerful, and free from swearing and scurrilous discourse, is worth gold."*) Nothing for it but to saddle up and wade right in; the situation is a bit similar to finding someone else in bed with your lover—a fatal compulsion draws you on to see the worst. Two fly fishermen, right in the current where, without any surface indication, it deepens into a long narrow run full of some of the largest, feistiest trout in the entire river. "How you doing, Doctor?" one of the fishermen shouts, as he starts a new cast. "Fine, Doctor, how you doing over there?" his friend shouts back. "Just fine, Doctor! You nail 'em, hear?" "Okay, Doctor! Hit 'em hard yourself!"

Ray and I are sitting on the bank taking all this in. "What does this mean?" I ask quietly. Ray shrugs. "Maybe they're doctors?"

Noisy ones. They shout back and forth in that macho small talk you hear a lot of on the river these days—it's as if everyone not only is being fed their lines from the Saturday-morning fishing shows, but have adopted the Southern accent to match.

Ray is crestfallen and angry; this is his spot more than it is mine, the one he discovered by many hours of exploration and the divining rod of his own splendid intuition. In all the times we've fished here we've never had company, so I'm pissed, too. What both of us suffer from, ultimately, is the fact that we're lucky or unlucky enough to have fallen in love with fly fishing many years before it became a fad, setting up that familiar and not very pleasant syndrome (seven parts protective jealousy, two parts sincere amazement, one part snobbery in reverse) of having the rest of the world discover something you've been in love with all along.

But that's not the atrocity. The atrocity is this.

Both men catch fish. That these are chub—that the fishermen loudly identify these with exuberant whoops of victory as trout—adds a little ironic frisson to our indignation, but does little to erase the scar. As they fish, they become further separated, so the younger of the two, the one with the waxed cotton hat, is now directly below us, backlit by the sun, which is still not quite clear of the trees on the New Hampshire bank.

"He's got something wrong with his neck," Ray says. "Watch."

I watch—and realize it's not a crick in his neck at all, but that he has his head tucked in tight toward his shoulder, holding by this pressure, as he continues to cast, a cellular phone.

"He's on the phone."

"On the what!"

Ray squints, sees for himself, blinks, blinks again, sighs—collapses backward in a faint that seems real.

Who's this man calling? His patients, telling them he'll be late? His friends, telling them where he is, feeding them the exact coordinates of his fishing position? He catches another chub now, reels it in while he continues talking, then, releasing the chub, bringing the phone down, presses in a number, sticks it back there against his neck, resumes talking. His casual absorption reminds me, more than anything, of a secretary talking on the phone as she polishes her nails.

A beautiful river, a perfect day, a tonic to the senses. All this means nothing to him—for him, it's just another in the endless series of places where he can be reached.

(Flash again to Father Izaak: "*And for you that have heard many grave serious men pity Anglers; let me tell you, Sir, there be many men that are by others taken to be serious and grave men, which we contemn and pity.*")

By the time anyone reads this, the phenomenon of fly fishers talking on the phone in the middle of the river will probably be old hat, with catalogs offering special waterproof models just for this purpose, your choice of camouflage or dark Orvis green. I realize that many people probably see absolutely nothing wrong with conducting business or making social calls while they stalk trout, or, to put it another way, feel vulnerable and disconnected if their phone isn't constantly in reach. I also realize that many people like to fly fish via the Internet, transform their favorite fishing spots into digits that are broadcast around the world. I realize there are guidebooks and videos available for every major river in North America, taking you by the hand and leading you pool by pool in great detail. I realize, too, that one of this country's most successful businesses is the manufacture and sale of electronic fish finders—that there are millions of people who, spending their working day in front of marching electrons, enjoy spending their leisure hours sitting in boats watching electrons fish for them.

I could have some ironic fun with this, or change gears and wax bitter; better, perhaps, to bite my tongue in silence and slink back toward the 1940s, where I belong. But there does seem to be one point in all this worth extracting once again: that secrecy, long considered to be among a fisherman's most characteristic and endearing traits, seems to be taking it on the chin these days, and I think it's time it was restored as one of the highest of fishing virtues.

Late yesterday afternoon, as we were eating dinner at the Wilderness Restaurant in Colebrook before going back out, still mad over the phone stuff, who should amble over to our table but a couple of fly fishermen I know casually from home.

"How's the fishing?" they asked.

"Great," I said (for we'd done well once the doctors had left). "Six trout each, decent size, all on top."

Their eyes lit up—it hadn't been a good day for them. "Where?" they demanded.

"Well, you go—" I felt a telepathic something in the air, hesitated, looked up to see Ray staring at me *very* intently; if eyes were feet, his pupils were kicking me on the shin.

"You go down—that way," and I pointed.

"That way?" they asked.

"Yeah, you know. Down that way by where the river is."

"Oh, that way," they said, and nodded.

All four of us sat there over our coffees not saying much, not having to. These were experienced fly fishers after all. They had probed, we had defended, so what else was there to say?

That someone who not only talks about the rivers he loves, but writes about them, is a bit vulnerable in the secrecy department is something, believe me, I'm fully aware of. In my defense, I'm known for including my share of protective obscuration; one of the most frequent responses I get to my books, when meeting someone who knows them, is having them shake their head, say something to the effect of, "That pool you call The Pet Store. I couldn't quite figure out exactly where you meant." *Damn straight you couldn't figure out where I meant,* I feel like saying. I'm dumb, but not that dumb.

(Regarding Ray's secret run, it's worth mentioning that I've made it up entirely. It's not on the Connecticut at all, not even in New England, not even in the Western Hemisphere; nope, not even on this planet, so there's no use your searching for it this side of heaven. That okay, Ray?)

So, my fellow fly fishers, the time has come to bring secrecy back into our gentle pastime—the tight lips, the polite shrug, the knowing wink. Be generous with your help to beginners, praise a river all you want, help strangers out with tactics and flies, try to show them by word and deed what fly-fishing ethics are all about, but when it comes to your favorite spots, cherish them in secret, keep your mouth shut—and leave the godamn electronics at home.

The New River (3)

Some lessons I've learned. . .

That there is a special way fly fishers talk about a river, see a river, regard it, that it is all but incomprehensible to someone who doesn't share our obsession. The argot of line weight, tippet diameter, a rod's pliability; tackle craft and the complicated minutiae that goes with it; the specialized references to insects, with their erudite flavoring of Latin; the shop talk of flies, referred to now by the name of their inventors, now by their descriptive nicknames, generating words that are as colorful and vivid as any in our language; the fascination with current and depth, bottom and cover, the geological lingo, the fluvial one; the calendar that has nothing to do with the Gregorian, but marks off the season in hatches, stream temperatures, water levels, and spawnings; the map, the vivid and raised map, of fishing success and fishing failure, superimposed over a graph of good days and bad, endlessly perused for its lessons; the body language of leaping hands, painful grimaces, melodramatic shudders—the puzzled frown, the slow rueful shake of the head, the shrug that says it all. All these contribute, so it's quite possible for two fishermen, comparing notes on a river, to talk in a language that to the uninitiated sounds as arcane as Greek, and yet to fly fishers is remarkably universal, an Esperanto of the fishing passion.

This language has only one goal: to speak of the river in a way that leads to the catching of more and bigger trout. The verbs, the nouns, the adjectives—all these are used like an abstract kind of fly, one we toss around fairly wildly at times, yet which must be chosen with intelligence and deliberation, carefully fastened to our purpose, thoughtfully delivered, attentively followed as it works its way across the water toward the fish it's meant to snare.

That the most important and vexing factor in fishing the Connecticut is water level. The upper part of the river drains a large and turbulent watershed, with tributaries that come down from high soggy plateaus on the Vermont side and snowy uplands on the New Hampshire, so in most seasons the river doesn't become fishable until the second week of June. Even then, things are dicey. It's a tailwater fishery, and the release from Murphy Dam is usually reliable enough that there is little fluctuation in the course of a normal day. No, the tricky things are the summer thunderstorms that can be remarkably isolated, and yet so violent they dirty up the river fast enough to eliminate all fishing.

We've learned over the years to expect these, keep our tactics flexible. Even if the weather has been good down here I make a point of calling Ducret's and asking about local conditions; all it takes is for whoever answers the phone to go over to the window and look out at Mohawk Stream, the tributary that runs right by the shop. It dirties up fast—but if it's clear, the chances are the main river is clear as well.

Even if we receive the green light, we're still faced with a two-hour drive to get there—time for a lot to change. If the water is high but clear, it's worth fishing, though there will be many places we can't reach; if it's dirty and brown, it's still worth prospecting to see if we can't get above the offending tributary, or, changing tactics, head downstream far and fast enough to beat the silt, get an hour or two of clarity before we have to quit.

If worse comes to worse, there are the tributaries to fish. Sometimes we'll drive up to the headwaters between the lakes, try there. If it looks like the entire river is up, we can bail out completely, head over to the Androscoggin, which is only thirty miles east—though this, of course, means raising the stakes for a long disappointing drive home if it turns out to be muddy there as well.

Low water can also be a problem, particularly in drought years like 1988 and 1995, or when the power company forgets its corporate responsibility toward the health and well-being of the fish. The river looks ugly and exposed at these times, and if hot weather kicks in you'll see dead rainbows. But this is exceptional—most years, July is perfect.

Between high water and low, there are at least five or six weeks each season when the river is completely unfishable, making for what is in effect a closed season within the open one—and yet when it's over, when the level goes back up or falls back down, the fishing can be the best of the entire year.

That partly because of the difficult, sometimes dangerous water conditions, partly due to the fact that it's inhabited by wild and moody trout, the Connecticut is not a river for beginners or the

casual once-in-a-whiler. It's a river that is constantly asking you to *reach*—reach with your cast, reach with your patience, reach with your wit—and someone who is inexperienced may find they're being asked riddles they're not quite ready to solve. The two most common fishing situations here are casting to rising trout in slow water where a single clumsy cast is enough to drive them sulking back to the depths, and fishing fast, turbulent pocket water where it can be hard not only to hook fish, but to even detect their strikes. Then, too, wading is difficult at the best of times; there's that high water which will hold the timid in close to the banks, or the low water where the rocks become covered with weedy slime.

Does this mean it's a river for experts? No, because in all my years of fly fishing I've never encountered an expert, have come to believe they don't exist. The good fly fishers I know are the ones who, competent with the basics, put most of their energy into many hours of local investigation; the *best* fly fishers I know add to this large resources of intuition, the kind of imagination that likes to tinker and probe, excellent vision, a gentle way with water, the gift of attention—or, in short, qualities that have nothing whatsoever to do with expertise, but everything to do with grace.

That a five-weight rod with backbone is what you want to be fishing with here. The Connecticut offers a lot of variety; a hundred yards of fishing might call for drifting midges in slow water at the top of the run, dredging stoneflies across the bottom when you reach the middle, flicking attractors in the choppy shallows where the current picks up. Because of the size of the river, the depth, you frequently get into situations where you've waded out to your limit, cast to your limit, and yet still need a few feet more—and the only way to do this is by having in hand some extra graphite oomph. I fish an Orvis Henry's Fork, their jack of all tasks, but find myself vowing each year to switch to a ten-foot rod, not only for the extra power, but to hold more line clear of the current and cut down on drag.

I've gone up and down in this respect, but always come back again to the five-weight. A two-weight is a delight to fish, but the trout are seldom close enough here to make it practical, and in slow water where the light line would work best you want to bring in trout fast so as not to spook the next one waiting on line. I've gone up to a seven-weight in high water, one of those stiff, expensive, high-tech jobs, but find it simply too much rod; it crosses that crucial border between stroking the river's back and flailing it.

And I always carry a spare—a cheap pack rod I stick in my rucksack with my lunch. Perhaps it's only me, but I find graphite rods surprisingly brittle—I've broken two or three in as many years. But then again, I'm an aggressive, absentminded caster, am always asking of my rods too much, and they tend to answer, with a little sighing sound, by breaking at the ferrule.

That when it comes to flies you would be well advised to carry a large assortment of the usual old reliables, but then spend all your time trying to discover which particular pattern the trout prefer as their flavor of the month. For there is a flavor of the month, or rather, a flavor of the season—we've discovered this again and again. What makes it interesting is that this flavor will vary from year to year so when you start on the river in June, last year's flavor means little and the search has to start all over again. ("You don't want vanilla? How about cherry vanilla? Maple walnut? My, you're fussy today, little fella. Mint chocolate chip?" . . . I bite my tongue, dig out another scoop, wait for that appreciative and greedy swallow.)

The first year I fished the Connecticut it would have been foolish to use anything on the surface besides small Light Cahills. For that endearingly reliable *stenacron canadense* was everywhere that year, and if they started to slow down in mid-summer, then something very similar took their place; it was as if the river were sending up an airy ginger-yellow froth to gladden man and trout. I came back the following season armed with dozens, but went the entire summer without seeing anything on the water but caddis—small brown-gray ones that came off the water in unbelievable numbers. Other years it's been the darker mayflies or caddis again, only this time in white or olive. I don't have enough entomology to explain this phenomenon, but whatever surface pattern you discover early seems to be the one you'll be fishing five months in a row.

There are some more specialized considerations. Emergers are worth trying; quite often, especially in slow pools with little current, you'll see trout rising to what seems thin air. For a long time I thought they were sipping midges, but even something as small as a 24 wouldn't interest them—they want a meaty emerger that never quite manages to break the surface film, and they want it fished with a tantalizing little twitch just as it comes into view. There are times when they *are* feeding on midges, and when this happens you might as well bite the bullet and go right down to a 22 or 24—18s and 20s are hardly worth bothering with. You would think it would be a good terrestrial stream, rushing past meadows overhung with trees, but in ten years of fishing I've never caught anything on a grasshopper or beetle, though I keep trying them, especially when not much else is happening. Every August there is a hatch of flying ants that lasts the length of one afternoon; I've always managed to be elsewhere that day, with timing that is impeccable.

I've had a lot of success fishing attractors over the years, though my friends laugh when I tie one on. To a generation weaned on match the hatch, these gaudy generic patterns are *infra dig,* the feathery equivalents of Big Macs . . . but I like them for that reason, spend so much time fussing, it's fun now and then to fish in sheer bad taste. The Royal Wulff is my favorite; it seems to provoke a response from trout that doesn't depend on color and silhouette as much as it does something chemical—if they want it, they *want* it, and I'll never tire of seeing that splashy all-or-nothing kind of rise it provokes. If Wulffs aren't working, I'll put on a Schroeder's Hare's Ear Parachute, which has the nice trick of vaguely resembling a caddis and vaguely resembling a mayfly, combined with that Hare's Ear kind of nondescriptness fish love. If neither of these are working, then I'll switch to a Yellow Humpy, more out of my perverse sense of humor than anything; I'm convinced fish strike it out of their own sense of humor (or to bulk up on roughage?), thinking it harmless, showing off.

More? I like Zonkers, but they don't work up here. Muddlers take hatchery trout, Woolly Buggers take natives. Hornbergs are a waste of time. Stonefly imitations are useful. Wet flies are definitely worth trying, too, particularly Hare's Ears or Cahills. As mentioned, the trout up here have a sense of humor, and appreciate a little movement in a floating fly; you should be fishing caddis sloppy, for instance, with all the crosscurrent drag you can muster. I've never seen a river where trolling works so well, by which I mean dangling your line absentmindedly behind you as you wade upstream. This always seems to get a bite, even from water you've fished carefully for an hour with no success. Why? No explanation, other than the trout's ironic take on life—and a trout's sensibility is nothing if not ironic, especially a brown's.

That it's a beautiful river to float with a canoe, taking you away from the road, away from the competition, in and under and through a tunnel of maple, ash, sumac, and birch, a bower of vines laced with moving water that is to the rockier, faster stretches of the river as the Amazon is to the Madison. Even if it wasn't for the beauty, a canoe can take you to water that can't be reached wading, especially those characteristically deep, slow, featureless pools that even to an experienced eye look fishless. In spring, there's enough inertia in the current so that you'll be fishing downstream all the way on a moving ramp that allows for no second thoughts, but later in the summer the current slows, and with a little paddling you can backtrack to spots you missed coming down or those pockets deserving of being fished twice. Still, even in these conditions you'll often be casting downstream to rising fish; this is extraordinarily difficult, especially when there's not enough current to give the fly any movement, so you have to drop it on their noses without spooking them. But what I like about a canoe (or even a drift boat) is that it makes you into an angling version of mounted infantry—transports you pool to pool in luxury, then lets you climb out and do the harder fighting on foot.

Spotting a canoe, shuttling around cars, can be an awful waste of time. Our trick is to lock a rusty old mountain bike to a tree where we're going to take out, and then the youngest, most energetic of the duo (defined as the one highest from catching the most trout) pedals back five miles to our starting point to fetch the car.

That on this kind of river with its wild, strong fish, it's insanity to fish with a 6X leader, hubris to fish with a 5X, prudence to fish

a 4X, caution to fish a 3X, sloth to fish a 2X . . . and optimism to fish a 1X.

That it's a good river on which to hit for the cycle, take a rainbow, brookie, and brown, even do it on three successive casts. The rainbows will be the most common of the trio—if you catch ten fish, seven will be rainbows, two will be browns, one a brookie. The best of these will be wild fish, which becomes apparent the moment you tighten on them—no stocked fish will fight like that. The river *is* stocked and stocked fairly heavily, but only in those spots where the truck can back up to the river without sliding in. This allows you to avoid the industrial fish entirely, not suffer the embarrassment of catching those three-pound brood fish New Hampshire likes to dump into the river to inflate its reputation—salting a gold mine that is already full of fish.

What fish these wild ones are! The rainbows thick and full-bodied, their pink taken up by muscle so it's more of an added enhancement than it is a definite marking, their gills having the healthy red shading you see on their cousins out West. The browns, butter-colored just like they're supposed to be, with that iridescent spotting I can never see without wanting to stroke. The brook trout, small but willing, the river's original inhabitants and so always welcome, particularly in autumn when the males, to my eye, take on the most fluid, delightful color nature can create—those coral fins, those copper bodies!

In all the years I've fished here I've never been able to come to a definite conclusion as to which locale each variety prefers. Browns, of course, are said to favor slow water, but I've also found them in the heaviest current, albeit with a rock or log nearby to absorb the worst of the brunt; rainbows, going somewhat against their usual grain, are the fish you find rising in those slow, lazy pools, even in summer; brook trout can be found almost anywhere, but seem to favor best those scooped-out hollows downstream of islands, where they'll congregate in happy schools, caper about like kids on recess.

That some of these fish will be big—that the Connecticut is a big-fish river, with all that implies regarding mystery and excitement and keeping you on your toes.

This is important. Many rivers have the gift of charm; only a few have the gift of depth. The Connecticut is one of these, and much of it comes from the sense you have, even without immediate evidence, that there are big fish lurking about. Those deep back eddies that, judging by their appearance (their swirling vortices that swallow branches whole, let alone flies) must be bottomless; the logs sticking out of the water like the sharp outerworks of an unconquerable fort; those stretches so fast and deep and unfishable they function like a combination wildlife refuge, nursery, and old-age home where trout may flourish unbothered by man. All these create a certain aura—and if they aren't enough, then there are those grainy black-and-white photographs that show up in the newspapers just often enough to keep things interesting: ten- and eleven-pound browns, held up by someone who's caught them on Rapalas or worms.

One morning last summer, fishing further downstream than we normally venture, my pal Ray Chapin caught four fish, two rainbows and two browns, the smallest of which was nineteen inches long. Had anyone else, I wondered, anyone else in the continental United States, fishing the same day, taken such a glorious quartet? I don't think so, and if you qualify that to east of the Mississippi, almost certainly not.

Hearing of these fish, seeing them on the end of someone else's line, drooling over those pictures, I began to feel more than a little bit left out. Here for four or five solid seasons I'd been working hard to get to know the river, grasp its secrets, and now I couldn't help feeling it was time for the river to repay my devotion and grab hold of me. A big fish would do nicely in this respect, acting as the emissary, the embodiment, of the depth and gravity I'd sensed in the river right from the start.

Knowing the next fish that takes your fly might be five or six pounds enhances the fishing experience in all kinds of ways. It makes you think much more about tackle, measure your rod and tippet in terms of what they can do against a really strong fish; it keeps you from taking anything for granted—makes you fasten on fish more gently, knowing what kind of power you might suddenly be attached to. It makes you scan the water differently, searching out places a big trout could break you off, readying yourself for chaos. Most of all, it makes you regard the river with a double focus, appraising it not just for where the trout might be hiding, but where the *big* trout might lie—the effect is that of reading one of those novels or poems that work well on two levels, the everyday and the mythic, so the river is acting continuously on your imagination, expanding it in airy fantasies even while it solidifies that expectant base.

And then the river did fasten on me, fastened twice, the second time hard enough even a slippery fellow like myself was hooked. It came about like this. . .

Ray and I were fishing some pocket water we hadn't fished before, working on the theory that on a hot summer day the trout would be hungrier and more active in current that was broken and oxygenated than they would be where it wasn't. For once, it turned out to be the correct assumption, and with the sun at just the right angle it was easy to pick up the quick, desperate splash-ings as the trout came up to chase, tip, and grab.

It was a good day to be out. The water ran in those broken surges of gold that brings out the kid in you, makes you happy to be alive. Ray found a chute where the water, hitting the road-block of a ledge, flowed in a channel perpendicular to the cur-rent's main thrust, and he was busy taking one small rainbow after another along the rim. I stayed out in the middle, doing just as well, the trout leading me upward pocket by pocket and ever so slowly across toward the Vermont side.

I was fishing a 5X tippet, a small, heavily greased Royal Wulff. I was also half-asleep out of sheer contentedness—with a twelve-inch trout sitting behind every boulder, I felt I could go on enjoying them all day. As I came closer to the bank I had to veer back out again to get past a heavy stretch of rapids; past this, I resumed my westward inclination, to the point where I was within casting distance of the bank. Sleepy, but with my instinct still working, I became aware that the pocket ahead of me and slightly to my left was much deeper than anything I'd seen so far—deeper and longer, so there was a ten-foot wide band of smooth water extending from an upstream boulder to the head of the heavy rapids. Again, acting purely from instinct, not quite realizing the implications, I tossed my fly over, expecting noth-ing more exciting than another twelve-incher.

The rainbow that came up to the fly was much bigger than that. The rainbow that came up from below the fly, reached for it, took it, and kept going through the surface film to the altitude of my forehead was a trout of four or five pounds. But here I'm already racing ahead of the moment itself. What I was aware of first was hardly its size at all, but a shocking and overpowering sense of *reality*—finding out reality, truth, was a hell of a lot dif-ferent than I had heretofore thought it to be; realizing I had been nowhere near understanding the river's capabilities to generate living, healthy, vibrant *flesh,* and that what I was now faced with was the sudden and overwhelming need to get back in touch with this new reality, at odds that, thanks to my casualness, were impossibly long.

Ray, who had been following me upstream, saw the fish jump and we both yelled together. It came back into the water flank first, making us both think (we discovered later when we compared notes) of the most ludicrous, yet inevitable analogy, given its splash—of a bowling ball dumped into the river from great height. *I must get below him before he reaches that rapid*—as in all violent situations, I was given an instant of remarkable clarity before things started to fall apart. On the first leap I managed to stay attached, but at the second—at the precise moment I remembered my tippet was far too thin—the tippet parted and that was that.

"Jeezus!" Again, we both yelled this in unison and—after standing there staring at the black hole carved in the river by the trout's escape—waded together over to the Vermont side, immediately starting in on the yearlong analysis called *what I should have done different.*

It was winter before the regret softened enough that I could see I'd done something right—found what was probably the best ten yards of fishing on the entire river, a spot we were calling the Trophy Hole even before we waded back out. Again, I couldn't get over how the smaller trout had led me over there fish by fish; it was as if I'd whispered, "Take me to your leader," and they had responded instantly. As for losing the monster—well, there was this consolation: it's almost impossible to practice catching fish that size, and if I'd made a crucial error it was in not recognizing the water's potential just by looking, and changing instantly to a heavier leader.

Armed with those most precious of weapons, hindsight and expectancy, I would catch him next year—or so I thought. All through the following spring the water was too high to let me get across to the hole, or even to tell where it was located in the bank-to-bank dance of rushing white peaks. It was the middle of July before I had my chance—a soft rainy day when the sky and weather blended into the same pewter grayness and anything seemed possible.

Tom Ciardelli was with me—he was the only one we had let in on our discovery. Still, he seemed skeptical . . . it was all that talk about bowling balls . . . and stayed downstream to fish the pockets while I plowed on upstream.

I found my way to the hole all right. I stood there gauging it, trying to figure out a game plan to use if and when the trout took again. The rapid below me was the crucial factor; no way could I hold anything immersed in its force. If I stayed on the outside of the rapid, though, I would have difficulty following anything in the treacherous footing of those rocks. After thinking about it for a while, experimenting with various stances, I decided my best bet was to plunge through the waist-deep current and get on the Vermont side of the fast water; if worse came to worse and I had something too strong to hold, I could step up onto the bank and follow him on dry ground.

I'd checked and rechecked my leader before starting and felt pretty confident in that respect. I had a Wulff on, since I wanted to repeat as nearly as possible every step that had worked last time. Nervous, knowing it was unlikely anything would come up the first cast, but knowing I had to be ready just in case, I worked out some line, then dropped the fly just below the boulder that marked the hole's upstream start.

The strike was instantaneous, solid and hard; I'd seen the snout appear below the fly and was already lifting up my rod when it took hold. It's difficult remembering which came first, my amazement that fate had come through again in such classic fashion, or my surprise that this wasn't my rainbow at all, but—as if by a miraculous feat of transfiguration—a large, a very large, *brown*.

I'll spare you the details of the fight, other than to say this: how delightfully rare it is in New England to fight a fish that is a *long* way off, making you feel like you're flying a remote-control airplane, something that's attached to you but remains almost entirely independent, so you marvel at being able to exercise even a modicum of influence. It was a powerful fish, but nowhere near as fast and dangerous as the rainbow; I had the sense, even as I fought him, that it was an old fish, a year or two past its prime. It got in the fast water just as I feared, but the second part of my plan worked to perfection; by hopping up onto the bank and hurdling various boulders I managed to stay below him and slowly led him over to a gravel shingle that sloped into the water as gradually as a boat ramp.

Tom, hearing me yell, seeing the commotion, had hurried up to meet me, and with his help we had it measured, photographed, and released in the space of a few seconds. Twenty-four inches from snout to tail, with a big angry hooked jaw, a yellow that was brighter than any I'd seen on a fish, and just a trace of slackness on what was still a fine, thick flank. That I was pleased to have found him goes without saying, but what pleased me even more was the feeling that the river had come through for me big-time. I had explored and experimented for a good five years, tested and probed in all kinds of weather, watched and observed, tried my best to divine its secrets, and here in the middle of a rainy July day I had at last been deemed worthy of initiation, been accepted by the river into its bright and wondrous fold.

A fitting end to my journey of discovery—and yet I can't quite end this here, feel reluctant to sever myself even temporarily from the river of delight that runs so strongly it's as if I can feel its energy pulsing through these keys. But in sharing the wonders of my new river I haven't yet mentioned my favorite spot of all, something that sits on the western bank a short distance downstream of the town of Canaan, Vermont, beside one of the river's best pools. It's a sewage-treatment plant, squat and unlovely, resembling with its cement severity and flat storage tanks a service station for UFOs, and yet from it, and from its cousins downstream, flows everything beautiful I've described.

The best landscaped sewer in the world. This was the Connecticut's reputation just a few years ago, when so bad was the pollution and neglect no one would go near it, let alone write rhapsodies in its honor. That this has changed is directly attributable to the enormous collective effort to win back the river undertaken in the late-middle years of this century, including the federal legislation known as the Clean Waters Act. A long story, full of villains and heroes, successes and setbacks, but one I'll draw a simple moral from, including with it as deep and heartfelt a thank-you as I know how to write. Ray, Tom, and I. The fishermen we've met on the stream. The canoeists, the picnickers, the hunters, and the birders. Our children and our friends. We're the first generation to reap the benefits from the efforts of the generation just before, and it's because the fight was made to restore the river to health that everything follows. The trout, the mayflies, the otters, mergansers, and moose. All the enjoyment, the mystery, and joy. Conservation works . . . that's the motto I'll end on . . . and the task it works best at is the creation of delight in the human heart.

PART THREE

Full Season

Cohorts

I CAME LATE TO FRIENDSHIP. Like many people who reinvent themselves after their teenage years, I was ruthless in cutting off the friends I grew up with, and it was a long time before I found anyone to take their places. Suffering badly from the form of egoism called shyness, with a stern and idealistic view of the novelist's task (Proust called friendship an abdication of the writer's duty and I fully agreed), I felt friendship was simply not on my list of life's requisites. When I eventually softened in this regard, began to feel the need for friends after all, life wasn't willing to accommodate me just like that. I was living in the country, cut off from anyone I knew, and though northern New England's reputation for iciness is in many ways unjustified, it is and always has been a place where friendship doesn't come easy.

The upshot of this is that for over twenty years whenever I went fly fishing I went fly fishing alone. I mentioned this in an earlier book and it won me a certain amount of pity—perhaps the reason I mentioned it in the first place. But I can say now that nothing in my fishing has changed as much as my habits in this regard, to the point where I now pal around with the best of them, have become, at least compared with my earlier standard, as gregarious as a Rotarian. Like a reformed drinker or ex-smoker, I feel compelled to mount a platform, testify to the evils of my former ways, and thank with all my heart the two men who are largely responsible for converting me from fly-fishing loner into fly-fishing friend.

First, a few words about fishing friendships in general. It's not as easy a relationship as the nonfisher might think, since anyone with a passion likes to approach that passion in a certain way, and so is apt to find anyone approaching it with even a slightly different style an impious heretic deserving an immediate auto-da-fé. I don't know how many times I've had people try to set me up with the fishing equivalent of blind dates—"Oh, you have to go out with Ranald, he just loves fishing!"—only to discover that Ranald and I come at fishing with a very different set of assumptions and expectations, so our day on the river is a disaster right from the start.

A fishing friendship is a hard and demanding thing—a good, lasting one something that is rare and priceless. So much goes into it. A tacit agreement on how much seriousness to put into the enterprise, how much fun; an admiration and respect for the friend's abilities; a competitiveness that is playful, not corrosive—the ability to tease and the ability to commiserate; a genuine delight in the other's successes; a telepathy that works even when you're far apart on a stream, so understandings about lunch breaks, quitting times, and meeting places always seem to take care of themselves; a shared willingness to put up with disappointment, not let it get you too far down; facing a certain amount of discomfort together, even danger, giving the friendship some of the enduring loyalty known by soldiers in combat; the ability, most of all, to be young together, if only for the space of an afternoon, to work like men or women at being boys or girls.

100

I met Tom Ciardelli after our wives had already become friends. In the same aerobics class together, they had discovered that both their husbands were passionate about fly fishing, thereby setting the stage for us all having dinner together, and—for this is the way the women pictured it as they burned up those carbs—the men to become friends as well.

I resisted—my first impulse toward any social invitation is to turn it down. I'm sure Tom resisted, too; I'd published a book on fly fishing by then, and it was easy for him to picture some egotistical know-it-all arrogant yuppie scum snob. But Celeste worked on me (there was talk about a private one-acre pond), Andrea worked on Tom (couldn't he steal from me some secrets?), and the matter was settled—we would be going over to their place Saturday night at five.

We surprised ourselves by hitting it off, at least after the first awkward moments. Tom was not a man who put much energy into the social graces, and I can be stubborn in this regard, too. What saved us was that all these greetings and introductions took place outside—that ten yards away, shining in the soft way of semigloss paint that hasn't quite dried, was a gray-green expanse of water, Tom's famous pond.

We walked over together, stood in the shade of a tall white pine watching as out in the middle of the pond trout rose toward wispy brown mayflies. I commented on how healthy and strong the fish looked; "There's bigger than that," Tom said, with a little laugh. He reached down in the grass for some fish pellets that had spilled, tossed a handful out, and for the next few minutes we watched a feeding frenzy that would have done justice to sharks. Talking about his pond led us to talk about other ponds in the area, then streams, then rivers, our separate experiences on each overlapping like the rings sent up by those trout, until without really thinking about it, standing there with our Molsons, we began a dialogue about fishing that is still going strong thirteen years later. And right from the start I was struck with one thing; that Tom is one of those surprisingly rare fishermen who admire and value trout on their own and not just as quarry, finding trout the one species that really speaks to them about nature and wonder and the large scheme of things, so it's quite accurate to say, without irony, that trout represent to them something spiritual in life, not just sporting.

Tom looks not only like the kind of man who would be good at fishing, but the kind of man who would be good at almost anything, as long as it involves hard, largely solitary effort. He's not easy to know—there's very little to read on his surface—but this is more than made up for by the kind of granite toughness you see a lot of in these hills, if not always in scientists of his caliber. Biochemistry is his field, pure research; like many talented people who live up here, he disdains the glitz and perks of a showy kind of career in return for being able to remain in the place he loves. He's of medium height, broad chested, walks in the even measured way of a good athlete (power volleyball was his game), and it's only his beard that gives any indication of his anarchistic leanings—he's not a man who has much use for the usual orthodoxies, not in politics, not in science, not in fishing. He and I are the same age, born within a couple of weeks of each other, and this has proven not the least of the strands that make up our friendship—the synchronization of outlook and expectation that comes between people who started out on this planet at exactly the same moment.

Before dinner was over we had made plans to go out fishing. There's a pond over in New Hampshire he wanted to show me; it was one of the few bodies of water he'd found that had a significant hatch of *hexagenia*, those humongous mayflies that drive trout wild. Since I had never actually seen one of these, I was more than happy to go along.

It was an interesting enough night, though I don't remember catching anything. Tom proved to be a good man with a canoe, and a generous guide; when we did see a rise, he maneuvered so I could get the best shot. I think both of us were a bit nervous those first few moments; okay, we both talked a good game, but how would we do when the money was on the line? Sitting in the bow, I found it hard to judge his casting style, though I did notice how gently his line landed on the water, and I was impressed by his ability to identify what minutiae the fish were taking. We broke for sandwiches and beer, then paddled around the shallows waiting for the *Hex* to show. And finally they did—eight or nine of them anyway, big and yellow, looking like swallows in comparison to the flies we'd seen until then, drying their wings with the kind of deliberately slow macho flappings you see in weight lifters, then taking to the air—to be immediately snared by *real* swallows, so not even one *Hex* managed to escape as far as the trees.

In the years since I've fished with Tom many dozens of times; we've covered quite a bit together in the way of river, stream, and pond, been skunked on occasions when we should have clobbered them and clobbered them in situations where by rights we should have gone fishless. I think we've grown as fishermen in the course of all this, not so much in our tactical understanding as in the delight we find in our sport. Like a lot of people who work very hard to get time out on the water, Tom was once apt to let a fishless day bring him down, knowing it might be a long while before he could get out again. Now he seems more relaxed in this respect, having learned to accept, even relish, the bittersweet kinds of defeat trout can toss at you—though they don't defeat him very often. Ten years ago, I wouldn't have dared tease him about losing a fish; now he kids himself, clears the air with the kind of loud clear "Damn!" that does the heart good.

He's one of the three best fishermen I know. So strong is my faith in his talent that I often shamelessly take advantage, feel perfectly comfortable, come late afternoon, with lazing on the bank while Tom checks out whether the fish are still interested.

"Anything showing, Tom?" I'll call, lying there in the shade.

"A decent rainbow over there by the bank. Want to try him?"

"With what?"

"Bluewing Olive."

"You sure?"

"Try it."

Yawning, moving slowly, I let myself be coaxed . . .

Tom has an even more important role: he acts as my reality checker. If he can't catch them, then I know they can't be caught, thereby absolving me from any requirement to try.

I've tried to analyze over the years what makes him so good—why he takes the most trout when we go out and usually the biggest. I think the chief of his gifts is a superb patience. And by this I don't mean the lazy kind of patience most nonfishers think you need, sitting motionless on the bank watching a bobber and worm, but an active patience that combines an energetic seeking and probing with an understanding that the rewards for these might not come all at once; a willingness, in other words, to wait fate out. This is the one trait that reveals the scientist in him; he does not like to leave a problem behind, but meets it squarely, determined to find a solution before moving on.

What this means, put him on the river, is that he concentrates on just one or two spots, working them thoroughly, blotting out from his consciousness the fact there's more fishable water just upstream or down. He refuses to give in to the easiest and most dangerous of fishing temptations—believing that the fish are biting just one pool away—but digs in and fights it out on turf of his own choosing. Me, if I haven't connected within an hour, I'm out of there; Tom, after an hour, is just getting warmed up, and—having noted patterns in the water, flashes, hints, threads—will be a more dangerous, sharper fisherman at the very moment when other fishermen begin getting sloppy, lazy, and bored.

Patience carried on a few casts too long becomes stubbornness, but Tom is smart enough to avoid this; stuck, at a complete dead end, he accepts it and switches over to a more improvisational, hunch-based kind of fishing. Last summer, floating the Connecticut, I was doing fair with Hendricksons, but Tom wasn't quite satisfied, and switched to a Blue Quill—not an unknown fly, but one few fishermen carry in their box, even an expert tyer like Tom. But it proved to be just the ticket—the slight variation in color between his fly and mine was enough to overcome all the trouts' inhibitions. I've seen him do similar many times: catch fish with the grain, then catch just as many cutting across it.

I admire Tom for all these talents, but what I admire most is the sheer beauty and grace of his casting. Tired of fishing, or even just glancing up between casts, I'll become totally absorbed in watching him work out line over a far and fussy fish—decide, not for the first time, that his casting seems a kind of elegant handwriting against the sky. Those forward downstrokes so precise and measured, like bold Gothic *I*'s; the great coil of script as the line comes back; that extended question mark it briefly becomes . . . and then the downstroke again, another signature letter added to the blue tablet on which his line falls.

It's casting of the old school, when a fly fisher's ability was measured not in how far he drove a fly, but in how effortlessly.

Tom's casting is wonderfully effortless, so, watching from the distance, you wouldn't think he was putting muscle into the process at all, so much as merely wishing the line forward, and wishing it forward in the most fluid and perfect loop nylon is capable of assuming. Not once have I seen him strain to complete a cast—not once. Yes, I've seen him make sloppy casts (though damn few), but these are only the natural little imperfections that, rather than spoiling great art, are its surest indications. He looks genuinely surprised at these moments—surprised, I think, that there turns out to have been effort involved in the process after all.

When you watch Tom cast you end up watching his hands, particularly his left one. Many fly casters will tug and yank with their left hand, but never quite manage to seesaw it into synchronization with what their right hand is doing with the rod (someone who looks like they're constantly tossing sticky stuff from off their fingertips is doing it too vigorously). Tom's left hand seems linked to his right one by some telepathic and infallible sensing, so with the most economical, even negligent of downward motions it's adding power, force, and speed while the right one handles direction. There's a weaving kind of motion to it; once in Switzerland, watching local women demonstrate the particularly difficult kind of hand looming they were famous for, I saw in the rhythmic sweep, sweep, and pause of their hands much that reminded me of Tom.

I don't think I ever fully understood how intensely he loves fishing, not until last fall when we finished the season together—a slow, regretful kind of day, both in the heavy, Brueghel kind of grayness that had possession of the landscape and in our knowing it was goodbye to the river for another eight long months. Tom's not a man to let his feelings show, and yet just once, as we got into his truck and started the long drive home, I heard him whisper, to himself and with more poignance than the words alone can convey, "Now I have nothing left to look forward to . . ."

He's a good man to fish with, Tom Ciardelli. I think if I were ever to look back on our friendship and try to pinpoint the moments that were best, I wouldn't remember any day in particular, but something that happens in almost all our days together. Tom will be working hard on his favorite pool, and I will have roamed upstream, checking things out . . . and then an hour or two later I'll be back again, or he will have moved upstream to meet me, and we have one of those fishing reunions that come in midstream, with the simple, even banal vocabulary that is familiar to anyone who ever divvied up a river with a friend.

"Any luck?" "Nope. Anything up here?" "A couple of brookies. Nothing spectacular." "I saw something. Down there by that log." "Coming up to caddis?" "Brown ones. You give him a shot." . . . which, I suppose, are the kinds of things fly fishers say when they can't say, "Hey, I missed you, pal! It's good to be together again, eh?"

There's lots men say without saying it directly. Three years ago Tom and I were fishing a tailwater river up north. We had called ahead and gotten the tape-recorded message on when the dam would and wouldn't be releasing water, and so felt reasonably safe in what was otherwise a dangerous enough position. We waded across a shallow channel to a sandbar where we could cast the rest of the way across the river; we had been fishing there not more than fifteen minutes when we both noticed something seemed different.

"Hey, Tom," I said, pointing to the rocks. "Am I imagining things, or is the water going back up again?"

Tom stared toward the stick we'd planted in the sand to measure any such fluctuation. "It's going up. Let's go!"

Instantly, without discussing it further, we started back across the shallow channel—the channel that was already full of rushing water as high as our waists. Tom, holding his vest high like a fussy old woman but moving powerfully for all that, made it across to shallower water, then looked back toward where I was struggling. My hat fell off—I grabbed for it too late—and then I realized I had a lot more to worry about than hats. The water was gaining vertically on my horizontal shoving—a second later and the current pushed my boots off the gravel and I began to be swept downstream. It was then I felt Tom's hand reach out and fasten on my shoulder—so strong, so secure, it's as if I can feel that same arm reach out and steady me now as I type these words, a tower of strength leaning out from that bank to bring me back to safety, to standing on the bank feeling relief and gratitude and admiration, and—because we're men—trying to express these things without using any of those words.

"Thanks," I finally managed, gasping for breath, the river pouring off of me. Then, scowling: "Why the hell didn't you save my hat!"

I've always had the feeling, watching Tom on the river, that I can understand quite clearly the talents that make him such a good fisherman. It's a different story with my other fishing partner, Ray Chapin. He's a marvelous fisherman, every bit as good as Tom, yet study and analyze his talent all you want and there will always be an aspect that *can't* be explained, at least not without sounding like a mystic.

We met at a party at a mutual friend's; I was sipping bourbon off to one side when a young man whose beard couldn't quite disguise a boyish, handsome face came over and introduced himself. He had read one of my books, was himself just at the point where he was abandoning spinning for the fly rod, and was full of questions. Ray is the kind of person you feel you know instantly; struck by the soft earnestness of his manner, much against my usual habit, I asked if he would be interested in trying out his new fly rod on one of my favorite local streams.

Ray is ten years younger than I am, so there was something of the master and apprentice in our relationship—at least that first time out. He was still clumsy with his casting, but after ten minutes of fishing I could see he had all the tools to be extraordinarily good. Athletic, sure-sighted, passionately interested, and a native Vermonter with a real affinity for the terrain, he immediately put me in mind of James's definition of a writer: "He on whom nothing is lost."

He was working two jobs at the time, as a draftsman designing houses and, on weekends, as an orderly in our local hospital so his family would be covered by health insurance. I admired him for this, his hard and continuing effort to reinvent himself—an effort that a few years later had him going to college with kids half his age, taking the opportunity he never had as a youngster to grab the learning he craved and deserved.

It's been one of the most rewarding things in my fishing life, watching Ray develop as a fly fisher, come into his own as a man who loves the sport and does it honor. I remember that first year fishing together up north, Ray rushing downstream to where I stood casting, a bow wave cresting out ahead of his waders, so excited he could hardly talk.

"There's something happening up there. You've got to come see!"

"Happening? Like fish happening?"

"I think it's a ha-ha-ha . . . a *hatch*!"

And that's what it was, the first Ray had ever seen, and he did just fine with it, though not without some coaching; when he turned his back on the river and started to wade toward shore, I yelled "There's one!", whereupon Ray hooked the trout backwards over his shoulder, spun like a matador, and brought him in.

He's a superb caster, with a good ten feet of distance on me, more if he wants to reach (he's a basketball player, and basketball players, spending long hours coordinating hands and eyes to work at distance, often make the best fly casters). He's tireless, often wins on the river from sheer endurance. Unlike a lot of fishermen, he's comfortable talking aesthetics, or sitting back and just drinking in the views (I remember once lying on the grass along the bank, the two of us watching spellbound as the crests of the birch trees high across the river became aglow with swarming caddis, so it was as if each tree were lit by a lambent flame of spontaneous generation). He's an efficient, businesslike fly tyer, especially with the patterns he's devoted to: the olive Hare's Ear, a little black nymph with a wisp of sparkle, a ratty brown caddis. I've seldom seen him fish streamers, though now and then, not without grumbling, he can be persuaded to chuck and duck with a Woolly Bugger. He can wade a river with a risky kind of prudence—there's no machismo in him, but he enjoys pushing the envelope of what can be crossed. And he's a fast learner; I've seen him make mistakes over the years, but never the same mistake twice.

As I suggested earlier, all these only partly explain Ray's success. He brings to fishing another quality, one I'd be tempted to call pure luck, were it not for the fact that the quality is much more reliable than luck alone. After thinking about it for a long time now, having seen Ray in action on all kinds of water from Maine to Montana, I've become absolutely convinced that in some subtle and yet compelling way fish *like* Ray, enjoy being caught by him, will seek him out in a river full of anglers, as if

they can sense that this is the one whose heart they should gladden first.

For Ray not only always takes the first fish, but always takes
the last—fish like saying goodbye to him just like they like saying hello—and almost always finds the biggest one as well. We've
fished Slough Creek together several times, have covered the
same pool with the same flies, alternating casts, and—the polls
are definite on this—the cutthroat prefer Chapin three to one.
The same is true on the Yellowstone or the Connecticut or wherever we fish. Ray would blush if he heard me say this, and people will probably think I'm nuts, but again it's the absolute truth:
fish like Ray and are forever coming over just to revel in his presence.

And perhaps because I've seen him do it so many times, my
enduring memory of Ray Chapin will be of him hooking still
another good trout. That quick upward glance that always manages to seem surprised; the instant switch to total, heron-like
concentration; the rod going up as far as he can reach; the
smooth and furious cranking to get the fish on the reel; that
instinctive first step backward into shallower water . . . and then,
without ever taking his eyes off the fish, the slow dance over to
the spot where he'll bring him in; the smooth reach back over his
shoulder for the net; the prayerful stoop to land him; the grate-
ful little shove of release; the long, half-wistful glance as the fish
swims off . . . and then the happy, embarrassed smile as he looks
up and finds me staring in absolute wonder once again.

The only regretful part of my friendship with Ray and Tom
is that so seldom do I get to fish with both of them at the same
time. Last September we managed to pull this off, all three of us
on Maine's Rapid River going after landlocks on dry flies. We had

spent most of the day on different parts of the river, but now, after lunch, we converged on that lovely slow pool where the river slackens into Pond-in-the-River. For a change I figured out the salmon first, called over to the other two what they were taking, but then the fish switched over to something smaller, and this time Tom was the one who picked up on it, and then a half hour later when they went back to something medium-sized and a different color it was Ray calling out the pattern, so between the three of us, communicating instantly, positioned in an arc, it was like we were holding a net between us and those salmon never had a chance.

Who's the better fisherman, Ray or Tom? Sometimes I play around with this, try imagining which one I would choose to wade out into the river to try for an extraordinarily large and difficult fish, knowing only one person would have a crack at him before he took off. Choose Ray with his instinct or Tom with his patience? I think about this, compare their approaches, and for the life of me I can never pick out which one would get the nod—and so, as in the case of all such ties, there's only one option left.

"Hey, Tom," I would say, glancing over to where he's stringing up his rod, all but drooling in anticipation of that trout. "Remember all those times I've paddled you around in a canoe, muscled us upstream just to get you in a good casting position? Remember those picnics I've thrown together, the nachos, the roast beef, the salami? Remember how I've always field-tested the concoctions that come off your tying bench, including those Clouser Minnows that are borderline legal? Remember all the books I've loaned you over the years, the times I've given you what turned out to be good advice?"

"Yeah, sure I remember," he would say, his forehead creasing up in suspicion.

"Hey Ray," I would say, turning the other way toward where Ray is tying on a caddis. "Remember who was responsible for introducing you to this sport? Remember all the times I've shared my thermos of hot tea with you, those cold rainy afternoons? Remember all the good fish I've stepped aside from to let you have your chance?"

"Uh, yes," he would say, frowning, beginning to catch my drift.

I'd have my own rod strung up now, my fly ready, my leader stretched tight. "Tom, Ray. You guys are the greatest friends a man ever had. I want you to sit here on the bank, relax in comfort, and enjoy watching a *real* fisherman strut his stuff."

And as my partners gape in admiration, I would wade out into the river and make friends with that trout.

July 4

I CROSSED THE DIVIDE, but not a great one. The road climbed just enough for me to downshift into third, then there was a level stretch, then it started down. Flashing out the window like little silver mirrors signaling me to stop was a stream hardly wider than a yardstick, but it was dropping westward now, not eastward like the stream I had been following up to the height of land. The sources of both were beaver ponds so close to each other that a child could lob a beach ball from one to the other without strain, and yet the difference was dramatic for all that, at least when it came to flowage, trendings, and ultimate destinations.

Behind me the water ran abruptly down to the Waits River, then straight ahead to the Connecticut, thence three hundred miles to the placid, overused waters of Long Island Sound. Ahead of me it flowed down by many windings to the Winooski, then to Lake Champlain, thence to the Richelieu River into Canada, north to the St. Lawrence, and down that river to the wild and tempestuous ocean off Newfoundland. Or, in other words, what was a difference of a few yards on a nondescript patch of green Vermont hillside became, give gravity time to operate: a global spread of some twelve degrees of latitude and nearly a thousand nautical miles.

It's the kind of thing I enjoy thinking about as I cross this little hump. I don't make the drive often, and when I do it's to fish the Dog River, my favorite medium-small stream in the state— a real charmer, whose wild fish are smart and pretty enough to make even a longer drive worthwhile. Water that stays clear and cool even in July; lush coils of vines and shrubbery that hide it under a tunnel; a rough-hewn frame of village, woodlot, and farm centered squarely against verdant hills. It's a stream best described as— Well, at the time I couldn't remember the exact word, though I was trying to. There's an old-fashioned adjective that fits the Dog perfectly, but for the life of me I couldn't come up with it, this being the only vexation in what was otherwise a perfect summer afternoon of low humidity and high nubby clouds.

I parked a hundred yards downstream from my favorite pool, then bushwhacked through the jungle of greenery that hides it from the road. I was betting July 4th would be an ideal time to fish—people off partying and the green drakes hatching right on schedule. I was right on both counts—no fishermen, plenty of mayflies—but here I'm getting ahead of myself, giving away the end before I've even gotten wet.

There's an odd quality to fishing the best Vermont trout streams; so perfect can be the surroundings that you blink and disbelieve for a moment that they're real. I pushed through the crisp mare's tails and sharp raspberry vines to a border of cinnamon ferns, then out onto the undercut gravel embankment that fronts the river proper. To my right the water ran down in a wide shallow chute that emptied into a pool deep enough for swimming; when I turned the other way I could see the rusty railroad bridge that crossed the river from bank to bank; past this, curving out of sight, was a choppy stretch of riffles that ran through high pine.

Lovely as all this was, it was only the inner core in entwined strands that were each beautiful in a different way. The surrounding farmland with its green corn that was knee-high, just like it was supposed to be on the Fourth; the two-hundred-year-old farmhouses that sat back on the first high land from the river; the railroad tracks, so serene now and forgotten; the sense all this gave you of a wise and responsible stewardship. Throw in some deer (a doe splashing across the river; its fawn shyer, staying on the bank until I passed), a red-shouldered hawk, a rare scarlet tanager (only the second I'd ever seen), some high-spirited trout, and you have a river that exudes the sense of well-being only the last best places on earth can.

Even the ambient sounds, usually so corrosive, only added to the overall effect. There was a tractor taking care of second haying, never mind the holiday; the distant laughter of people playing miniature golf in a simple course a farmer had put up on his spare field; the chesty booms of fireworks even more distant, even happier, a pleasant staccato in the lushness of the prevailing tune. Here for the space of a summer evening the world was staying at exactly the right distance; I hitched up my waders, shook my head to stir up the perfection some, eased my way down the bank into the light, skipping pressure of the stream.

Has anyone ever written in praise of ankle-deep rapids? They're delightful, both in sound and sensation—the smooth-moving sheen, the way your wading boots break it apart into foaming runnels that don't reform until twice your shoe size downstream. The Dog, at least when it's flavored by a setting sun, is the color of mild chamomile tea, and that amber quality was most pronounced directly at my feet. Again, and with the same vexation, I tried remembering the word that describes the river's murmuring quality, but it still wouldn't come.

By the railroad bridge the streambed is littered with old granite blocks left over from the original construction; they've been there so long now they've become a yellowed part of the natural landscape. The rainbows like to hide in the slow water behind them, getting up the nerve with excited little spinnings, then dashing out into the current to swipe a fly. As mentioned, these are wild fish (the Dog hasn't been stocked in thirty years), and they show it the moment you hook one. Never—not in catching salmon, not in catching bass—have I seen fish jump so high proportionate to their size; an eight-inch fish will shoot out of the water so fast, so high, your head snaps back to keep it in sight. Pyrotechnics! The analogy, with those boom-hiss-booms in the background, the flaring arcs of the rainbows' parabola, is both fitting and inevitable.

After catching five or six of these, I eased on downstream, on the lookout for the drakes, trying to appraise the changes in the streambed since the last time I had fished here. These were considerable; there had been two destructive floods in the course of the spring, and a deep pool where the river hooked left was gone entirely, its bottom filled with gravel that had been deposited when the current hit the bend. I accepted this with more grace than I would have thought possible, considering it had been my favorite pool; in the give and take of floods the pool just below had been scoured out even deeper, so most of the trout had simply migrated twelve yards downstream.

The green drakes were beginning to show. As with a lot of things in fly fishing, they're not really the color they're called, but a parchment-like yellow. They're big, too. The largest Cahills in my box, size 12s, were too small to match them, though the trout—stuffed, on the lookout for lighter servings—took them readily enough. It had been a while since I had seen such a ful-some hatch on such a small stream, and after catching another rainbow, the biggest of the night, I stood hip-deep in water enjoy-ing the way the flies appeared out of nowhere on the surface, dried their wings for a moment, then, with feathery little inhala-tions, took to the air like Valkyries made of papyrus and dust.

Time to move on, fish one last pool before dark. There's another old bridge site, this one much rougher and forgotten, with only a moss-covered abutment on one bank and a vague indentation in the cliff on the other to show where a cart track had once crossed. You can't wade through the pool without spooking all the fish, so the only thing to do is send a fly down from above, bouncing it off the cliff, then tossing in some slack so you get a few decent inches of drift. Browns predominate here, but they seem made of the same exuberant stuff as the rainbows, leaping to incredible heights. In the twilight, with green drakes everywhere, they weren't hard to catch, and I hoped to find a big trout before it got too dark to fish.

For a moment I thought I saw one, the largest trout in the river, swimming downstream with the wiggly, nose-first grace of a harbor seal. I wasn't far wrong, at least in my analogy. It was a beaver, one that surfaced now right below me and gave a tremen-dous thwack with his tail. On any night but the Fourth I might have been considerably pissed at him, putting the fish down like that, but as part of the overall celebration his cannonade fit right in. He gave me four or five of these thwacks, each a little closer; he swam closer, too, to the point where I could have jabbed a boot out and spun him around. He (or more likely she) wasn't motivated by the usual kind of territorial imperative, for on the next pass through the pool she seemed to separate into three parts, one larger, two small. Baby beavers, the first I'd ever seen, no bigger than eight-week-old retriever pups, and just as curious, tumbly and tame.

Trout, beaver, tanagers, mayflies. The distant sounds of celebration. Not a bad way to spend a summer evening. If the setting was perfect, my little jaunt through it had turned out perfect, too, so I didn't feel separated from the landscape, but a deep, essential part. A removable part, of course. In the darkness I waded back upstream, the trout rising so freely now it was as if they were trying to nudge candy loose from my pockets. They put circles in the river's downstream surge, made the water take on even more of that quality I felt so thoroughly, yet still couldn't name.

But then an hour later, driving up over the divide toward my own familiar valley, remembering the color of the water, the even, melodious way it flowed, I came up with the right word in a flash of inspiration, so sudden and satisfying I beeped my horn twice to match its syllables: *purling*. A purling river, the Dog is. A veritable purl of watery delight.

Save the Fountain

I'M A CENSUS TAKER for our local streams, an unofficial, self-appointed one, someone who likes to keep track of how many wild brook trout still grace our small corner of the planet with their habitation. I go out in all weather, three seasons of the year, armed with the traditional tools of my avocation: an old fiberglass fly rod with three missing guides, a patch of fleece with half a dozen flies embedded in the marl, Polaroid sunglasses scratched and stained from long usage, a scrap of paper, a stub of pencil, and, most important of all, the long and puzzled questionnaire that passes for my brain.

As best as I can determine, there are seven wild brook trout currently residing in our town: three in Slant Brook at the base of a small waterfall where the stocked trout can't bother them; one in Whitcher Stream where it bounces down to the Connecticut; a hundred or so in Trout Pond up on the slope where our mountain begins—trout so tiny, so miniaturized, you could put them all end to end and still only count them as three.

Not many fish, of course, but perhaps the miracle is that there are any left at all. Twenty years ago, when I moved to New

Hampshire and began my survey, there were hundreds of brookies in all these locales—enough that the counting of them kept several dedicated census takers working full-time. I'd come upon them in the woods, secretive men apt to shy away at your approach, stubby rods pressed under their arms, their faces greasy with fly dope, favoring dark green work clothes, the only splash of color being the bandannas around their necks. Interesting men to talk to if you found 'em in the right mood; theirs was an intimate association with the landscape and its creatures, and they were less apt to talk about entire rivers or streams than they were individual pockets, boulders, and holes. Most of them valued wild trout greatly, yet possessed one self-destructive habit: they thought of their subjects as food—and not just for thought.

These men are largely gone now. If the trout are down to seven, then the census takers are down to one—me, probably the last one in the neighborhood who realizes wild trout are still among our inhabitants. I've taken to wearing green work clothes myself now, that same red bandanna, honoring by imitation a dying kind of breed. And even I don't go out surveying as much as I used to—I'm tired of walking, knocking, and finding no one is home.

But here I am veering off into bitterness when a census taker should stick to the facts. The trout I know best are the three in Slant Brook. This is as typical a New England trout stream as you're likely to find. Starting high on the side of our town's one steep mountain, it plunges down through the forest in an exuberant rush of brightness, sluicing westward through the uplands, carving a channel for itself through granite bedrock, dropping over two sizable waterfalls and the ruins of old mills, crossing under the highway in a giant culvert, then taking on new life as a meadow stream in the last mile left to it before joining the Connecticut in a marshy bay.

The lower three miles have trout in them, lots of trout, for two weeks a year. These are brook trout that have been raised in cement tanks in another part of the state, transported here by heavy truck, poured into the brook where it meets the road, caught immediately by people who fish no other time of year, the trout that survive being swept downstream by the first heavy rain, to end up as pike and pickerel feed in that marshy bay mentioned above. Stocking fish has been going on so long now in this part of the country it's become part of the natural order of things, so you have to step back a bit to realize how odd, how truly bizarre the whole business is. I mean, phony trout? Cement trout? Trout from the city turned loose to entertain the rubes?

I encounter these trout sometimes in the course of my rounds, and am appalled, not by their meekness, but at their savagery. They strike a fly with desperate fury, turn quickly if they miss and strike it again even harder, as if from an impulse that is homicidal and suicidal at the same time. Catching them, you feel like the butt of a cynical and expensive joke, the kind you see played by art forgers or the worst kind of cosmetic surgeons, those who think beauty is for manufacture and sale. That there is just enough color and energy in these trout to convince the gullible that they *are* real makes the joke more bitter; it's only in comparison to the genuine article that the forgery becomes apparent.

Here's where the miracle comes in. Despite hatchery trout, the nearness of the road, wanton destruction of shade trees, the way the brook's most important tributary is looted for snow-making by our local ski area, the sloppy leach fields of too many houses, the penchant previous census takers had of eating their subjects—despite, that is, every wanton and cruel trick man can play on it, Slant Brook still manages to harbor at least three genuine wild brook trout, huddled together in a thirty-foot stretch of habitat like genuine flowers in the middle of a plastic garden.

How wild trout manage to survive here is partly a matter of luck, partly a testament to what, despite their fragility as a species, is an individual toughness that is as much a part of them as their beauty. A few yards downstream of the looted tributary, replenished by what water trickles in, is a pool no larger than a dining-room table, formed by water falling over a burnished log. A plunge pool you call this—the coolest spot on the brook, thanks to that turbulence, and cooled even more by the shade of a pear-shaped boulder that sits on the bottom a foot or so from the lip of the impromptu weir. Upstream of this there is nothing but shallows for a good hundred yards; downstream are more shallows, so the pool, in brook trout terms, sits like an oasis in the middle of a desert. It's far enough from the road that the stock truck goes elsewhere; it's shady, deep, quiet, forgotten, and in its center live the last wild trout the brook contains.

I've only interviewed these fish, face-to-face interviewed, two or three times. I pride myself on my restraint, claim it's for conservation reasons, but the truth is they're remarkably hard to catch. The stream is hemmed in by brush, making casting difficult. The trout favor the three feet of water between the fallen hemlock and the boulder, so you have a yardstick's worth of drift when they might possibly take your fly. Unlike the stocked fish, they won't rise more than once, and there's much more discrimination in the way they bite—not that greedy boardinghouse grab, but a delicate kind of aristocratic plucking.

They're beautiful, of course, drop-dead beautiful, and already in August have begun to take on that rich purple-red blush that speaks so eloquently of autumn. Only eight inches long, they have the thickness of flank you see in the healthiest wild fish, along with an iridescent luster that makes it seem they are taking the granite sparkle of the brook, the verdure of the forest, the dappled sunlight, mixing it all, internalizing it, then through a magic I never get tired of witnessing, generating these qualities back in their purest eight-inch essence, so holding a trout in your hand, for the seconds it takes to release it, is like grasping nature whole.

The biology of it—how three or four fish manage to survive and reproduce in what is otherwise a desert—mystifies me, and all I can do now is pay tribute to the fact that reproduction, growth, life, does go on here, without any help from man. The Slant Brook trout demonstrate one possibility for the native brookie's future, albeit a tenuous one—living in isolated, forgotten pockets but flourishing there, like cloistered monks working on illuminated manuscripts through the worst of the Dark Ages, their most beautiful, vivid illumination coming from within.

Whitcher Stream, four miles to the south, offers another possibility. Similar in size to Slant Brook, it begins in a chain of beaver ponds in the notch between two steep hills; in time of high water the edges of these ponds lap the rocks of old cellar holes from vanished farms. A meadow stream in its upper reaches, it veers south into our neighboring town, then—as if not liking the neighborhood—immediately swerves back again, finishing its last mile to the Connecticut as a rocky, shady stream with numerous deep pools. Prime trout habitat—and yet to the best of my knowledge, only one trout remains in the entire stream.

It's a native trout; that's the only good news in what is otherwise a depressing enough story. The state stocks only one stream per town, and so any trout in Whitcher Stream is perforce a native. Ten years ago there were hundreds of fish here, two or three in each pool, but each autumn when I went back, there were fewer and fewer, to the point where there's only one left now, in the deepest, most brush-tangled of the pools—a pool that seems, such are the implications, the haunted graveyard where the last of a species goes to die.

I caught it last year and I'm sorry I did. It's an emaciated fish, with the kind of pale, muted coloration you see in creatures who live without hope. This, of course, is anthropomorphism of the worst sort, but there you are—it's impossible to understand what the last trout in a river must feel without taking into consideration what must surely be a cosmic kind of loneliness. For a moment I was tempted to put it out of its misery, break its neck with a little pressure of my hand, but I found I couldn't do this. If the trout in the brook hovered on the point of extinction, I wasn't going to be the one to give them the final shove, or at least pretend I wasn't, me who drives a car, consumes too much energy, accepts too meekly the prevailing order of things.

Nowhere else in town do I feel such a direct connection between the fate of trout and the fate of man. The Whitcher family after whom the stream is named, among the first settlers here once the French and Indian Wars ended, is down to one surviving male member—a young man of nineteen who was just arrested for what in some respects was a meaningless crime: shooting at a minivan with his deer rifle. He's been sent off to prison for this; am I the only one in town who senses a linkage between his fate and that of the Whitcher Stream trout? Dispossession is dispossession is dispossession, no matter which link on the chain snaps first.

There's lots more here for our local census taker (taking a break at our village lunch counter, staring down at the one wretched check mark scribbled down on his pad) to mull over. Alongside Whitcher Stream, on a grassy level patch above the ruins of an old box mill, sits an unusual kind of development. Our local millionaire, as sort of a hobby, bought up decaying old houses all over New England, had them trucked here, then reassembled them in a cluster of upscale offices, shops, and an expensive private school. The backdrop of all this is the stream—valued for its scenery, its atmosphere, but otherwise ignored.

The irony of this hardly bears underlining—that so much effort and money could be poured into rehabilitating a portion of New England's past while the *living* symbol of that past, the wild brook trout, is left to die out without anyone noticing or caring. And there are other ironies in this line. Over on the Connecticut millions have been poured into a salmon-restoration effort that, sadly, has shown very little signs of having worked. All this money to bring back something that's been extinct here for nearly two centuries, and not one penny spent on preserving the salmonoid that's been here all along, leaving to future generations the hard task of restoring it, an effort that will undoubtedly be as futile as trying to call the salmon back with our impotent whistles of regret.

And this, I suppose, is the Whitcher Stream possibility for the brook trout's future: the river as background noise, local color, pretty dead stuff, inhabited only by chub, water spiders, and millionaires.

To write about a third possibility for our local trout I may have to swerve over into magic realism. The eastern part of town is a wild, high province of softwood forest, beaver meadows, and bright open ponds. One of the largest of these is Trout Pond, reached by a half-hour hike along a shaded woods road the years have pressed deep into the earth. Forty years ago the pond was poisoned by the state to "reclaim" it from the trash fish, then stocked by helicopter with brook trout fingerlings. This was a very fifties kind of operation—the helicopter, the faith in technology, the belief in the quick fix. And yet it worked—for a time. When I first moved here and discovered the pond (it's hard to find and the locals kept their mouths shut when it came to directions) the trout had established themselves as a self-sustaining population, and—if you could lug in some sort of boat—you could count on several fat fish over twelve inches, coming up with discrimination to the tiniest of flies.

This was *not* a fly-fishing-only pond; fishermen would dump their bait buckets in the pond when they were done fishing, and a new generation of "trash" fish grew to maturity with those brookies. For a few years both populations maintained a rough sort of balance—and then suddenly, in some ecological battle too obscure to follow, the chub got the upper hand, so they were everywhere, huge ones, attacking a fly the moment it landed so you could hardly keep them off.

As the chub flourished, the brookies declined. I caught fewer each time I went, and found their size was declining, too, so an eight-incher became a real trophy. The good news is that the town obtained control of the pond and saved it from development; the bad news is that no one has the slightest idea how to reestablish the fishery as it once was. Poisoning is out in this day and age, and my own suggestion—backpacking in some chain pickerel to act as hit men on those chub—hasn't won much support either, for the obvious reason: those enforcers are just as likely to eat up the good guys as they are the bad, finish those brookies off once and for all.

What's going on up there is very odd. If you were to have asked me two years ago I would have sworn there were no trout left in the pond at all. I went back anyway last October, lured by the beauty of the pond itself (no mirror reflects foliage better than those three level acres of gray-green glass), and decided, such is the force of habit, to bring along my rod. Someone had dragged in an old aluminum skiff and tipped it against a pine where the inlet comes in. It reminded me of the *Merrimack*— there were bullet holes everywhere, some perilously close to the waterline—but I decided to take a chance. Using some broken hemlock limbs for paddles, I managed to coax it over to the cove on the pond's eastern shore.

I didn't catch fish, not at first, other than those hateful chub. The problem was that my imagination was totally out of sync with the pond's reality; it was still picturing twelve-inch trout, or eight-inch trout, and fishing accordingly. A couple of hours went by . . . I was at the point you can get to too fast in this day and age, when the beauty of the surroundings begins to deflate without some vibrant life at its core . . . when I noticed a vague upswelling in the water by a sunken log—not a rise so much as the ghost of a rise. I searched through my fly box for the smallest pheasant-tail nymph I could find, tied it on with some 6X tippet, then sent it out to see if it could summon that ghost.

It could. Something nudged the wind knot in my leader, then came a tug on the fly itself. I lifted my rod in a reflex gesture—and then ducked as a fish came shooting back toward my face.

This was a lot in the way of gymnastics for a trout that turned out to be two inches long. A brookie, beautifully formed but all in miniature, so for the few seconds he lay in my palm I had the uncanny sensation I was looking down at him through the wrong end of binoculars. Clearly, this wasn't a baby trout but a mature adult—a male, judging by the spawning colors, the vague jut in the underside of its microscopic jaw. I cast the nymph out a little farther and immediately caught another one, a female this time, Mrs. Tom Thumb, just as perfect, just as small. Realizing that two-inch fish were what I was fishing for, I scaled back on my notions, began looking at the pond differently, saw that what I had assumed were the disturbances left by water spiders and caddis were actually bona fide rises—that there were dozens of trout left in the pond after all, at least in this one deep cove.

Good news and bad. Good in that I was pleased for purely linguistic reasons there were still trout residing in a place called Trout Pond; bad in that the race had become miniaturized, so it was hardly correct to speak of them as gamefish at all, but rather as the miniature markers used in a game, toy trout, nostalgic centimeters. And yet I admit I enjoyed catching them, felt these germs of trout create a germ of delight in my eyes, hand, and wrist.

I've been thinking about these trout a lot over the winter. Obviously, the chub are crowding them out, making it impossible for them to find enough food, stunting their growth. But it's hard not to think that the trout are up to a deeper game. It's as if they've deliberately decided, from motives of self-preservation, to become small and smaller, thereby escaping man's attention altogether, to flourish on as a race of midgets no one bothers catching. Trout as leprechauns only the fortunate ever see? Yes, something like this. Philosophers of an earlier age insisted everything evolves toward pure spirit, and this may be the local trout's only salvation, to ruthlessly shut down whatever gene controls growth, evolve into something that is little more than a brightly colored minnow, the bonsai of salmonoids, ignored, unsought for, but at long last *safe*.

Thus my survey, the three possibilities for the familiar neighborhood brook trout of rural New England. Hermitage, extinction, miniaturization—and a fourth possibility I've not explicitly mentioned, but that underlies all my hopes: that mankind (or at least the concerned part of it known as fly fishers) realizes what treasures are on the verge of being lost and spearheads an effort to bring our brookies back, quite literally, into the mainstream of local life.

Census taking, while meant to be a precise science, has built-in limitations, and my methods are not infallible by any means; surveying with a worm, for instance, would undoubtedly result in a more accurate tally, even as it killed my subjects off. Then, too, any census taker, even one who's been at this game many years, has their instinctive biases, and these must be taken into account in digesting their reports. My own bias is this: I believe the native brook trout, the wild brook trout, *Salvelinus fontinalis* (which in my pidgin English becomes *save the fountain*) is the quintessential New England creature, the one whose health or lack of health best reflects the health of the natural world here, the being upon whose slender back— not to put too fine a point on it—the whole health of our rural culture depends. Without brook trout, a stream is dead no matter how pretty it looks from the highway; beauty, dead, turns ugly very fast; ugliness, piled high enough, corrodes the soul. There must be a thousand streams in New England capable of supporting wild brookies. Stripped of them, these form a thousand cemeteries, complete with headstones and the keening wail of empty water. Graced with trout, they become springs of delight, reservoirs of solace, fountains of well-being—and not just for trout.

But then census takers aren't supposed to get so involved with their subjects, draw any conclusions from statistics alone.

I count, the number is seven, and unless things change dramatically, in a few years the last lonely searcher through these hills will be able to do all his counting on the trembling fingers of one gnarled and arthritic hand.

Fishing the Millennium

I KNOW THE MAN WHO HELPED invent fly-fishing schools. This, in his defense, seemed like a good idea at the time. He was working for Orvis back in the '60s, a decade when fly fishing was at something of a low ebb, at least in mercantile terms. It was a sport your father did, or your grandfather—the baby boomers were too busy exploring other options. What better way to stimulate sales and interest than by holding weekend seminars in which the fundamentals of the sport were taught? Get students casting with instructors, have some lectures on entomology and flies, take them to the river and talk about streamcraft, then give them some time to roam loose about the tackle shop. Great idea, right?

Thirty years later the answer is yes and no. Randy himself doesn't fish much anymore, at least on his beloved Battenkill; the crowds, many of them graduates of the Orvis school or one of its imitators, line up three deep on the banks every June to wait for their chance at eight-inch fish. Randy shakes his head over this, rues the irony of his having been at least partly responsible. If in the '60s he was one of the smart, energetic young men on the cusp of fly fishing's boom, he's now one of those burned-out cases you see a lot of today, those who *used* to fly fish, but have been driven away by the mobs, with nothing left but stories of the good old days, their poignant and sterile regrets.

Sometimes I'll see these schools in action—an instructor wading down the middle of the stream followed by eight or nine acolytes dressed in neoprene and pile. They remind me of a mother duck and her chicks, charming and harmless, though at other times—times when, frowning, they stay in close to the bushes and superseriously *stalk*—they make me think of a patrol in the Mekong Delta, up to no good at all.

But then I'm a self-taught fly fisherman, have the scorn of the autodidact toward everything academic. There's something vaguely unseemly about seeing grown men and women still in grade school—everything seems out of scale. But when I get control of my prejudices I realize I'm of two minds about the whole enterprise. Surely these people have every right to enjoy fly fishing as much as I do; certainly it's a difficult sport to learn by yourself, and what harm is there in getting some coaching?

When it comes to the larger picture, the huge explosion in fly fishing's popularity of which the schools are partly cause, partly effect, I'm much more uncomfortable, to the point where I have to fight through all kinds of emotions before I can even begin to comprehend the avalanche that has caught us old-timers unawares. Avalanche? Yep, a biggy, when the mass of snow that lay undisturbed for generations began to creak and groan and shift along about 1978 or so, gathered momentum in the '80s, then swept on down the mountainside in full irresistible force. Here at the century's turn *everyone* is fly fishing or talking about fly fishing, fishing vicariously on television or the Internet, signing up for expensive trips, going to fishing school, crowding up our rivers, wearing fish on their T-shirts, their baseball caps, their jewelry, the trout turned into a totem, the fly fisher, at least when compared with his older, rather comic and endearing persona, being in like Flynn.

How does this kind of mass longing come about? How does a sport for loners and traditionalists and the few suddenly become yet another fad in the massive, exaggerated way of American fads? To go back to the avalanche simile, it would take an expert on snow pack to give the correct reasons, but some factors are clearly visible, even to an amateur like me.

Spinning peaked in the '70s; after that its chief allure, its mechanical simplicity, became its chief drawback in an era when a lot of folks were looking for the challenging way to do things. Then, too, fly-fishing tackle was being improved by the introduction of new fibers, so the challenge wasn't *too* extreme. Hunting was taking it on the chin as a morally incorrect activity, so the catch-and-release aspect of fly fishing (a blood sport without blood) exerted a strong attraction to those who would otherwise worry about the philosophic implications. Norman Maclean's brilliant novella *A River Runs Through It* and the movie made of it did a lot to glamorize the sport, giving it not only a trendy literary respectability but a glitzy Hollywood sheen. Women were demanding their place on the water—a genuine, grass-roots kind of movement. Saltwater fly fishing kicked in with the return of the stripers to the Northeast. Ted and Jane were seen fly fishing—with Jimmy or Dan or Tom, or whoever was the celebrity of the moment. Once the avalanche started rolling, of course, the hucksters were there to throw in their own snowballs, swelling the mass, smoothing its way with their facile lubricity.

Anyone who's been around for a while has seen many fads come and go, from guitar playing to windsurfing. Many sports seem to go through a boom when everyone does it, then a point where only the diehards are left—cross-country skiing for example. Many of those attracted to fly fishing by its faddish allure (*you too can have this epiphany*) will surely drop out when they discover—despite the fishing schools, the assurances from the tackle companies—that it is indeed a very difficult sport to master, providing gratification that is far from instant and often no gratification at all. This is what my fishing partners long for, a crest to the wave, a gradual diminuation, so we can have the sport once again to ourselves ("I think it's crested," they'll say, when we find three fishermen on our pool, not seven). This may certainly happen; you have to wonder if there is enough water or fish out there to sustain this kind of mass attack. On the other hand, many cultural and sporting booms seem to die out a bit, then start up again in a second, even larger wave, so the worst may still be yet to come.

The saddest part of this has been the commercialization of a sport that should offer a refreshing antidote to commercialization. A modest dose of material interest has always been one of fly fishing's subsidiary delights . . . the old cluttered tackle shop; the catalog crammed full of gadgets . . . but, as with so many other things, it becomes a matter of scale. Soon, thousand-dollar rods will become de rigueur for all of us; already, reels come in at three hundred dollars, and that's not counting an extra spool. Magazines, the worst of them, create fly-fishing "personalities" who are then used to sell things no one needs, and even publications having nothing whatsoever to do with the sport feature fly fishing in their ads, using it to move everything from Jeeps to whiskey. (In the old days, if you saw a fly fisher in an ad, guaranteed he was holding the reel wrong side up; nowadays the ad men are slicker and everything looks authentic, albeit far too prissy and neat.) Fly fishing, like so much else in our culture, becomes a mystique that's for sale.

American consumerism at full throttle is not a pretty sight. A good many are confused by all the glitz, yet attracted to the sport just the same; they sense something spiritual may be had in being out on a river, something they can't find anymore in their boardroom, their bedroom, or their church. These are the pilgrims, and it's hard not to sympathize with them, even while, on their way to Canterbury, they let themselves be fleeced.

Between them, the nabobs and the pilgrims, they've created a new style of fly fisher, one who wants gratification *now,* and is willing and able to spend plenty in order to accomplish this. Three hundred dollars a day for a guide, plus tip? No problem. Argentina, a lavish lodge, an imported American guide, a picnic hamper with three varieties of wine? Sign me right up. These men and women are very serious about their sport, grimly so, and, managing a joyless competence, building their resume of rivers, they're always in a rush toward the next experience waiting on line, and have time to neither smell the flowers nor practice the ethical niceties of fishing etiquette.

Just a few days ago, as I was working the river under a hot midday sun, a couple of the new breed blundered into my pool. One came in directly opposite me and maybe fifteen yards away; the other, the one with the teal-colored vest, came in just below me on the same side, giving me the ominous sense that like professional hit men they were deliberately boxing me in. In the old days etiquette would have required they ask my permission before venturing into either spot, or that they sit on the bank waiting until I had fished through the pool (the same etiquette demanding that I do so with considerate regard for their patience). Of course, they didn't know about this, or perhaps they did, because neither one said anything to me at all, or even acknowledged my presence.

"Hello." I said it quietly at first, then much louder. "Hello!"

This got the one opposite me to turn; he glared, remembered he wasn't supposed to know I was there, put some surprise in his expression, managed a weak little wave. Sharing a pool with two boisterously eager interlopers is one thing, sharing it with two sullen time-servers is something else again, so I reeled in my line, went back to the bank, and started through the meadow downstream.

An unsavory incident now became something worse. Having fished the pool for all of five minutes, the two darted back into the woods, got into their Jeep, drove downstream in order to beat me to the pool I was walking toward; they were already out there flailing away by the time I arrived, having positioned themselves so there was no room left for me to fish, even if by this stage I had still wanted to.

Thinking back on this a few days later, I'm of two minds. Okay, idiots exist, in whatever sport, whatever pastime you care to name. Perhaps they were merely ignorant. Perhaps they fish so seldom, have so many pressures on them back at home, that they'll do anything to catch a fish. Perhaps their fly-fishing school was a little weak in the ethics department. Perhaps they've read one too many of the ads or magazine articles, have bought into the competitiveness that has infected our sport (and yes, competitiveness was praised among the highest manly virtues in that little book of Mr. Maclean's). Perhaps . . .

Well, I can think of a lot of excuses for them. But there's one thing I can't excuse and that's the grimness with which they went about their fishing. Whatever else these fly fishers were, they were *not* men who were enjoying themselves, and it's this new sullenness, this new competitiveness, that's poisoning our sport, not merely its sudden popularity, not merely the numbers.

I would like to think that none of this affects my own enjoyment. I would like to think I could continue to fish the forgotten corners in the solitude I love, write my little essays of personal celebration, not have to worry about larger concerns at all. But any man or woman fully engaged in this enterprise will find they often fret and worry about the condition of their sport, eye new developments warily and with inherent distrust, so perhaps it's not inappropriate to do some speculating in this line, if only as a kind of personal therapy, wondering out loud what the hell is going on.

And what better time to draw a deep breath, take a look at the state of things, then at the change in millennium? Fishing antiquaries like to push back the dawn of fly fishing to remoter and remoter dates, instancing pyramid drawings of fishing poles with what appears to be yarn or feathers on the end, the prototype fly. But for all intents and purposes, it's a method of catching fish that was "invented" sometime in the first millennium after Christ, perfected through the long centuries (with increasing speed during the last two hundred years), and is now standing poised to enter its second thousand years with far more practitioners than it has ever known before.

At first fly fishing was valued for its *taking* qualities—the fact that when trout were feeding on the prolific insect hatches of spring it was far and away the best means of taking these fish from the river for food. Quite early in its development (at least as early as Charles Cotton, writing in 1676) it was discovered that there was a lot more to it than this taking power alone—that it was an extraordinarily interesting, graceful, and challenging sport, one that, with time, became increasingly divorced from its purely fish-taking function. By the eighteenth century it was caught up in the aristocratic sporting tradition, where doing things the hard way, simultaneously increasing the difficulties and simplifying the means, was seen to be the highest sporting virtue. The American contribution to this . . . the peculiar genius of American fly fishing . . . was to take this highfalutin sporting notion and make it available to everyman, the aristocratic grafted onto the democratic. Written up by a boisterous sporting press and several brilliant popularizers, blessed by the raw material of seemingly unlimited water and fish, American fly fishing became where the action was in the sport; in fly-fishing terms, like so many others, the twentieth century was going to be the American century, where everyone got their shot at it, at least while those supplies of water and fish lasted.

The American century is over, of course; what this means, in terms of fly fishing, is that we're witnessing a perversion of what made our sport so special, a clash of the worst qualities of both traditions rather than a symbiosis of the best—the aristocratic hauteur and snobbiness taken up by a greedy democratic mob. It's tempting to say that what American fly fishing needs is a heavy infusion of the older, purer aristocratic values, at least as regards fishing etiquette, where fly fishers who pride themselves on doing things right would disdain to enter a pool someone else was fishing, sneer in contempt at all the hucksterism, find interest in figuring things out for themselves, take their greatest pleasure from leaving the smaller environmental impact consistent with their presence on the river.

What we need—what we need constantly—is to remember why fly fishing is worth doing in the first place. The difficulties and pleasures of mastering a demanding craft; the reinforcement, the enhancement, provided by a long and proud tradition; the solace of its locales, the inspiration these offer; the healing power of water; the miraculous living beauty of the trout we seek. All these things, and with them a quality that is harder to define—an anti-establishment kind of plea-

sure; the different drummer aspect that makes its practitioners favor the lonely places, doing their thing away from the
crowd, independently . . . the quality about fly fishing that has
always appealed to the dissident part of us, that stubborn nonconforming raffish heretical freelance something that even our
materialistic culture can never quite snuff out.

Perhaps this is why so many fly fishers feel uncomfortable
with the current boom: fly fishing simply cannot afford to
become too fashionable and still possess this alternative kind
of allure. Let's remember that ours is a quiet and simple pursuit in an age that is noisy and complex; one that rewards
patience and prudence in a jittery, impatient world; a sport that
requires thinking and creativity in a culture that often punishes
both; a pastime that seeks to conserve the places our money-
grubbing, joyless economy seeks to destroy; a soothing antidote
to everything in the world that so bitterly goes down.

Whosoever would be a fly fisher must be a nonconformist. A
paraphrase of Emerson, but one that fits.

Confronting the problems fly fishing is faced with as it enters
its second millennium is in and of itself part of the solution; its
adherents are a literate and intelligent bunch, highly motivated,
and merely by their keeping one honest and critical eye cocked
on their sport much healthy course-correction will inevitably take
place. There are ideas we should continue to think about. The
ethic of catch and release; an insistence on the primacy of wild
fish; stressing a low-impact style of outdoor etiquette; the effort
to preserve land through trusts and conservation easements; the
heavy-duty political battle of restoring the purity of our water and
air. Much has been written about this; much, in spite of serious
and well-financed opposition, has been accomplished.

More remains. Fly fishers have done a good job in fighting for what they love, but the brutal fact is that our future depends on our culture's attitude toward the entire natural world—the whole terms of our existence on this planet, and not just the sporting fine print. That our attitude must change and change dramatically to preserve what resources are still left goes without saying; that growth and exploitation and needlessly skimming off the earth's bounty without thought for tomorrow threatens a lot of things beside fly fishing is, again, so obvious it hardly bears mentioning. And yet even today this message has trouble being heard. That the economy is growing—that more resources, human and material, are being exploited at an ever-faster rate—is still considered by the movers and shakers who control things the very best news possible, though in reality it's often the worst. The writers and social critics who are talking about setting limits, changing our exploitative philosophy, are the ones doing the most to preserve our fishing, though they may never talk about fishing at all, may even in extreme cases look upon it caustically as a blood sport whose time is over. There's an attitude of *taking* we must hastily abandon, an attitude of *putting back* we have to speedily adopt, and it's on how soon this transformation takes place that the future of our pastime depends. We've had fifty years of warning. Only a Pollyanna, a liar, or a fool would think we have fifty years left in which to act.

And in this direction I'd like to suggest the adoption of a new fly-fishing motto, one that supplements the familiar "Catch and release." *Put, not take*—a slogan, a commandment, that should constantly inform us, and not only when fishing. Put fish back when you catch them, of course, but don't stop there. Order some willows or alders through your local nursery, plant one every time you go to your favorite stream. Put those fishing schools on an entirely new foundation, so they offer scholarships to local people or interested teenagers, help broaden fly fishing's demographic base to the point where garage mechanics are doing it, not just CEOs. Put some thought into fishing etiquette and whether your presence on the river, your manner there, is causing it harm. Put more effort into forming coalitions with other groups that are similarly motivated to save the natural world, and forget about all the various differences that otherwise weaken us—let the birders lie down with the duck hunters, the fly fishers make pals with the bass boys, so united we holler up a storm. Put those new masses to work, so we don't rue fly fishing's popularity but harness it, thinking of all these newcomers as valuable, badly needed reinforcements. Put aside the whole mind-set of *taking* that has infected our sport since its earliest days; start thinking about what we can give back to the river, not just what the river can give to us.

There's another practical idea that should be considered in the light of this emerging philosophy. *Put ten back*—a slogan that would urge fly fishers to place a voluntary tax on themselves, contribute ten dollars to conservation organizations for every time they go out fishing. Certainly, this would be a modest enough tithe, considering that American rivers can be fished free of charge. Followed faithfully, boosted by the fishing magazines, made easy by the establishment of statewide chapters to handle the cash, it would result in an enormous amount of money to be spent on conservation work of the most direct, pragmatic kind. In line with this I'd urge the introduction in this country of a vocation long established in Europe, that of *riverkeeper*—a man or woman resident on each of this country's major trout streams who functions as a combination watchdog–caretaker–public relations specialist–ombudsman–researcher–teacher. *Put ten back,* use the money to hire knowledgeable and dedicated people to live beside our rivers, and this alone would be a major step toward the moral and financial investment in our future this sport badly needs.

And a last word for those of my friends who complain that fly fishing has been ruined. Yes, some will be appalled by the mob, find they're too fastidious to deal with its pressures. Many—many of the sport's best and most faithful practitioners—will quite literally give it up. Some will retreat into nostalgia, become collectors of tackle and trinkets, hardly ever venture out onto a stream. Some will cope by fishing less, others by loudly complaining—the cynical, bitter fly fisher is someone you will meet more and more. Some, finding their local trout stream too crowded, will save up for the airfare to Montana; others, finding Montana too crowded, will dream of fishing in Russia, hope they can get there before Russia becomes too crowded, too. Some, maybe even most, will get used to the new pressure and adapt, finding new interest and energy in fighting to preserve their rivers, so there is more fishable water for everyone.

Me, I'm going to try to find in fly fishing's new millennium what I've always found in the sport—the miraculous current that connects simple pleasure to great joy—and try ten times harder to put my delight back into the river from whence it all springs.

PART FOUR

Trout Country

The Grand Tour

BOZEMAN, MONTANA, boasts my favorite airport in the world; a late August afternoon is my favorite time to land there. The sun will be low enough to give the mountains that surround it the kind of purple-gray color that brings them into sharpest relief, hints at majesty and mystery both, so anyone sensitive to mountain scenery, pressing their face against the window to see better, will find their adrenaline rises as the plane descends, the two emotions battling in that turbulent zone between the esophagus and the heart until they all but choke from sheer excitement.

The airport itself enhances this mood—it's one of the few I know that seems a natural portal to the experience you've come so far to find. Its low, low-keyed architecture contributes to this, with its suggestion of a comfortable bunkhouse; so do the decorative bronzes of grizzly bears, mountain men, and trout. Down by the luggage ramp a drift boat is displayed, making it seem as if you could start your fishing trip right there if you wanted; most of the people getting themselves sorted out have rod cases under their arms, and the ones who don't, judging by their clothes, the exuberant way they fling their arms around the suntanned women waiting to pick them up, look like they're headed back home to the ranch.

I'm traveling with my pal Ray Chapin this time, and for me it's something of a comeback. When I landed here in 1988 the great Yellowstone fires were raging, and even downtown Bozeman was covered by clouds of heavy, sweet-smelling smoke. An interesting enough experience, one in retrospect I wouldn't have missed, but as a fishing trip it was a disaster, and I'd spent the years since plotting my return. Ray, for his part, hasn't been in this part of the country before, and he's even more eager than I am to get our luggage together, fetch our car from the rental lot, find the quickest, most direct route to West Yellowstone, get rolling.

If Bozeman seems the welcoming portal to the classic Montana trout-fishing experience, then Highway 191 seems the yellow brick road that leads to its heart. Just south of town the mountains close in, the sky darkens, and to our left out the window is the Gallatin, looking cold and high in a late-afternoon shower. We've been talking over our plans for more than a year, and yet only now, face to face with the rushing foaming cascading reality, do we really start bringing them into focus.

"I want to fish it all," Ray says, pointing not just toward the Gallatin but toward everything that lies beyond.

"We could try," I say. "Not all of it, but a good chunk."

Pumped up by the altitude, those high peaks out the window, that Western sense of limitless possibility and expanse, we make it our plan: to fish as many rivers as we can in our week and a half, think of the trip as a grand reconnaissance wherein we'll learn as much as we can about as many rivers as possible. It won't be a race either, at least not a sprint; we'll think of it as a gentle half-marathon, and if we find ourselves rushing too fast, we'll deliberately slow things down. Eleven rivers in eleven days? There's a nice ring to it, and why the hell not?

A last meadow stretch of river, the height of land where the park cuts in, and then we're driving through the semideserted streets of West Yellowstone, scoping out the tackle shops and breakfast joints, noting with interest the drift boats parked in the driveways, searching for the cheapest, quietest motel in town. We finally find one, not far from the park's entrance. Cheapest? Maybe. Quietest? Nope. Right across the street is what turns out to be the rowdiest bar in West Yellowstone—but that's okay. What I'm determined to do this trip is give my imagination free play, and that means letting the little boy in me indulge himself in all the Western playacting it can handle.

Impelled by this mood, our imaginations strumming out some lonesome, twangy kinds of chords, we mosey on downtown. The loiterers outside the bar eye us with both curiosity and disdain as we walk past, as if we're hired guns with big reputations they're more than willing to cut down to size. It puts an *amble* into your walk, this kind of thing. We pick out a shop that seems reasonably authentic, hand our money over, and come back wearing cowboy hats pulled down to what we hope is exactly the right angle over our eyes.

"Howdy, boys," one of the loiterers says, stepping aside.

Howdy, boys. We are *here*!

River One: Grayling Creek. It's miraculous there's any daylight left in what already seems a double-length day, but there is and we take advantage of it to go fishing. Over to the park entrance to get a fishing permit, back to Craig Mathews's fly shop to buy a state license, then the short drive to Grayling Creek, that friendly tributary stream that plays peekaboo with the park's western boundary.

I fished Grayling during the autumn of the fires, since it was one of the few streams (with a hysterical governor having slapped a ban on all outdoor activities in the state's domain) that was both legal to fish—it's partly inside the park—and safely accessible. It's a pretty stream, just the right size to get us started, and with the kind of pool-riffle-pool alternation we're familiar with from home. There's lots of timber in the creek, fallen lodgepole pines, and they form an interesting network of jams, sluices, and undercut runs. In the near darkness, that adrenaline still pumping, we fish a little faster than we should— and yet the fish are there for us. That these turn out to be brook trout is both a surprise and an ironic kind of teaser—brook trout, after all, are what we have in plenty back in Vermont.

An hour of them and there's just enough light to get back to the car. We're tired, but pretty high. We woke up in our beds back in New England and now here we are finishing up a night of Montana fishing. Talk about your magic-carpet rides! At the edge of the creek I kneel down and splash some water on my face just to prove to my jet lag it's really true. And it is true. I close my eyes and shiver with it, that sense of traveling so far, the exhilaration of having crossed a continent, felt every one of those miles of prairie, wasteland, and foothill as a kind of adventure . . . so far, and yet in some mysterious, essential sense, coming via those miles to a place that is also home.

River Two: The Madison. Anyone who travels much knows the whole experience can often present itself as a series of questions. Where shall we eat breakfast? Try the eggs or the Texas French toast? Decaf or regular? Fill up with gas now or take a chance on finding some later? Cash the traveler's checks at a bank or save them for the motel? And which motel? Do the waterfall or the scenic drive? Which way is the rest room? Which exit do we take? Where's the turn?

To all these question marks the fisherman brings dozens of his own. Which river to try? Which pool? Which fly? Top or bottom or in between? Which boulder to cast to? Which side of the boulder? Twitch it or let it drift? There are thousands of decisions to be made, pretty much taken for granted at home, but once on a fishing trip they present themselves in capitalized italics, especially on a trip with no fixed itinerary when you're traveling with a friend and these decisions have to be reached in collaboration.

"Where do you feel like starting?" I ask Ray over breakfast.

"The Madison would be nice. Or we could head right into the park."

"We're both anxious to get going there. But maybe we should fish outside the park first, then have Yellowstone to look forward to."

Ray knocks back the last slug of coffee, waves to the waitress for our bill. "I'll try wherever you want to try."

"Wherever you want is fine by me," I say, reaching into my wallet for the tip.

We could go on this way forever, Marty and Manny talking over how to spend their Saturday night, but after about a dozen of these exchanges it becomes obvious that what we're both thinking about is the Madison outside the park. So be it. We go across the street to a bakery to stock up on snacks, stop at a convenience store for juices, decide that we're temporarily all set for flies, then turn down Canyon Street and start north on Highway 191 out of town.

The Madison flows out of the park and under the road—a glimpse and a tantalizing one, but it's not enough to stop us.

Where Highway 287 swings west to follow Hebgen Lake the trees give way, the mountains spread open toward the divide, and for the first time we get that characteristic Western vista of drop-dead beauty and heart-stopping expanse. Hebgen Lake contributes, even though it's manmade; it's like a mirage it's so flat and still, the sight of float tubers—fly fishers with their bottoms cut off, hanging in what seems pure air—only adding to the effect. Where the mountains pinch in again comes Quake Lake with its dead, branchless trees. An eerie, haunted place, the land sliced sheer, so it's as if the earthquake that formed it happened only seconds before we arrived.

I pull some seniority here; I can remember reading about the earthquake in the newspaper when it happened, before Ray was even born. I remember how exotic the place-name seemed, *Mon-tan-a,* the difficulty of trying to imagine what it was like when an entire mountain slid to one side. There are trout in the middle, judging by those rise rings, but even now it's not a place I would feel comfortable fishing—nature here is in its scornful mood, and you'd feel that dislocated mountain, the dark powers that still lurk below it, watching you on every cast.

And then the highway drops, the spillway gushes out an enormous fountain of bright water, and the mood instantly changes as the Madison, the real Madison, the river everyone dreams about, plunges down into the channels at Slide Inn, gets its act together, and roars in choppy riffle-osity toward Ennis thirty-eight miles away.

We park downstream of the side channels, pull our waders on in the morning chill, then walk over to the bank, awed as we should be awed—this is Augusta, Wembly, the Eiger, the big time.

"What a river!" I say.

Ray nods, squints, then points. "What a fish!"

My first impression is that a helium balloon is drifting on the water where it edges against the bank; my second, that the river has sent a special emissary to welcome us. It's a trout, a twenty-five-inch rainbow, a dead one. Surely an omen, but of what? The impressive size of the fish we're pursuing? The ominous fact that all is not well here (at this point in time neither one of us has heard of whirling disease)? Our best guess is that it's a fish that was played too long or was clumsily released—but its size, its appearing instantly like that, gives us a second, even stronger shot of adrenaline.

The riffle aspect of the Madison can be hard for a newcomer to adjust to, and we're no exception—for that first morning we kept looking for the pools. I flush a good fish right against the bank, which should have taught me something, but we persist in fishing those vague slackenings out in the middle. At home, the fish lie behind the boulders, not in front, and we're slow picking up on this. There are some caddis about, and a few times we think we see a rise, but these are hard to pick out in the broken, windblown water.

A slow start. Back at Slide Inn to get some coffee we meet a couple of fishermen who are just getting into their car. Men in their seventies, in that kind of khaki good shape that suggests ex-military, enjoying each other's company, having a great time, judging by their smiles—the kind of old-timers Ray and I wouldn't mind being someday ourselves.

"Well, you gotta remember two things, boys," one of them says, after we sing our little song of not much luck. "First is, all these fishermen you see, all the drift boats. Most of them can't fish worth a damn, so don't feel shy about going in after they leave. The other thing is—"

His partner finishes for him. "They're there. You might not think so, but the trout are there."

Good basic advice—and it becomes our motto for the entire trip, trotted out every time we face new water without a clue about what to do with it. *They're there;* you're not fishing over empty water, and you've got to act like that with every cast. And yes, we do much better in the afternoon, moving downstream toward Lyons Bridge, waiting for the drift boats to pass, then stepping into the shallows and fishing like every twenty-four inches of water holds twenty-three inches of fish. I catch my first one (a modest brown, but I'm amused at his pretension), and hold it up for a picture; a few casts later Ray catches a rainbow and it's my turn to snap him. We're chucking and ducking with black Woolly Buggers, nothing fancy, but at least we've discovered that the fish like to hold not only in front of the boulders but also in tight along the banks.

I relax more with each fish, begin to pay attention to the surroundings, the osprey soaring brown and white over the trees, the blue, wedge-shaped mountains on the horizon to my right, the grazing horses, the exuberant rushing sensation the river gives you that you're being swept along toward happiness whether you want to go there or not. Ray has been watching the water, gauging it, working up the nerve—and there, he hitches up his vest and wades right across to the opposite bank, making a dangerous, strenuous feat look easy.

We break for lunch at the Grizzly Inn, indulge ourselves in double hamburgers and double pilsners, feel pretty rosy by the time we go back out. We finish the day on the short stretch of water where the river powers out of Hebgen Lake. There's a wide side channel where you enter from the road, then a faster, deeper stretch past a narrow island; by the time we pick out good positions the air is dusted up by tiny brown caddis. Here we stumble upon our second good source of advice. A younger fisherman this time, short, wiry, a blond cowlick leaking down from his Stetson, he's all but bubbling over with suggestions, every one of which we later follow, every one of which turns out to be right on target. Who wouldn't listen to him? He is a natural, and as the three of us sit there on the island talking things over he glances up at the water, says, "There's one," roll casts out a caddis, and hooks an eighteen-inch rainbow he leads into our laps.

River Three: The Firehole. And advice is what we're talking over at breakfast this morning; what we've managed to garner so far is forming a stepladder against the mountainous stack of our ignorance. Perhaps because there are simply more good fly fishers in Montana than elsewhere, or perhaps because they're more generous with strangers, we're finding it's worth asking almost anyone for suggestions, including our waitress. Plates balanced on her suntanned arms, in a beautifully husky voice that has a good bit of Patsy Cline, she tells us her boyfriend works as a guide and that his favorite river is the Firehole, hands down.

The Firehole has the reputation of being an expert expert's river—the boyfriend must know his stuff. We fish the stretch known as Biscuit Basin in intense and windless sunshine, so it's not surprising we get skunked. For once it hardly matters. We're out here to learn, and that humility turns out to be part of the lesson is eminently reasonable. Skunked—but who cares! Who, standing in a gin-clear river that winds its way in lovely sinuosity through a lush meadow that hasn't changed since the white man first saw it two hundred years ago, a meadow that features on its upstream edge an aroused elk with his head stretched out making a sound unlike any other we've ever heard, a deep, siren-like wobble that is so rich and lonely and molten it must be coming from the center of the earth, using the elk as its bulging mouthpiece . . . a river, for that matter, that curves in and around hot geysers of white spray that suddenly spasm skyward and take on all the colors of the rainbow in cresting, shivering, draping apart . . . who, taking all this in for the first time in their life, could possibly ask that in addition a trout come over and shake their hand!

We see them anyway, holding under the fringe of meadow grass that forms a floating cover over one of the straightest runs. Beautiful fish, and maybe before our trip is over we can come back and fish a cloudy afternoon when something is hatching, at least stand a chance.

Our morning on the Firehole does manage to convey an important lesson about Western fly fishing. The difference between here and back home is one of not only scale, but degree. In the East, an experienced fly fisher will often reach the water's limit as regards trout before he or she reaches their own limit as regards ability; out West, you're much more likely to reach your own limit as regards ability before the river's limit as regards fish. We thought, quite frankly, we were pretty good; the Firehole began teaching us how much further we still had left to go.

River Four: Nez Percé Creek. In Yellowstone you have three or four hours of morning tranquility before the elk jams ("There's an elk, Edna! Stop the car!") begin to form and driving becomes impossible. Walking, you only need a hundred yards and you're free of the tourists, the RVs, the crowds. We're hiking up Nez Percé Creek for several reasons. One, we need something simple this afternoon after the Firehole; two, I love tributary streams; three, this was the route the Nez Percé Indians followed on their famous flight through the park in 1877, and we want to get a sense of what this was like.

In its lower reaches the creek winds through open meadows similar to those along the Firehole, sans geysers, but a mile upstream the pines close in, the shadows tighten, and the stream flows through a gently graded forest. Many of these trees are blackened leftovers from the great fire, little more than vertical chunks of charcoal, and it's a wonder they still stand. A wonder, too, that the fire didn't take everything; we spend a lot of time speculating about what trick of wind or rain spared some stands of trees and destroyed others. A light green carpet of vegetation underlines even the most devastated parts of the forest, so all that talk about regeneration is true.

The fish aren't hard here—nice rainbows, feisty and willing to take our nymphs. It's good to have the creek to ourselves; good to play leapfrog as we go, me in front for a trout or two, then Ray forging ahead while I slow down to work one of the deeper pools. After lunch I find a shady spot and try taking a nap. It's the first time I've ever been alone in the Yellowstone backcountry, and thus the first time I've ever really thought about grizzly bears in the way they're *meant* to be thought of—as splendid embodiments of all we cherish in wilderness on one hand, and ferocious beasties that can eat you on the other. It adds a frisson of uncertainty to even a catnap like this, and yet isn't this the point? To take man down a peg or two from his top-of-the-food-chain kind of hubris and strut?

There's a noise in the woods behind me, the splitting creak of timber. Ray? Oh Ray? Is that you, Ray?

Yep, it's him, nothing like a bear at all he's grinning so much. "Thought you were a grizzly," he says, putting his hand over his heart. "Nice stream, huh? You see those little bluewings?"

Back in town that night I stop in a bookstore and buy a couple of books on the flight of the Nez Percé. Eight hundred of them, led by Chief Joseph, Looking Glass, and White Bird,

crossed over to Yellowstone Lake following the north bank of
Nez Percé Creek (as it later came to be called), taking with them
a captured group of tourists—an English earl, two women, a
music teacher, a brewer, and someone history records merely as
a "blowhard"—who, needless to say, must have had the surprise
of their lives. I find two aspects of this story incredible: that this
was a national park that early and that you can imagine without
any difficulty what this long column of warriors, ponies, women,
and boys must have looked like as they passed, so little has the
landscape changed in one hundred years. Isn't this one of the
secrets of Yellowstone's appeal? The time-traveler aspect? Blink
and it's 1877, and if the grizzlies don't get you the Nez Percé will.

River Five: The Bechler. "Hey, Ray? You know Nelson Algren, the
old Chicago novelist? His rules about living, like, for instance,
'Never eat at a place called Mom's'?"

Ray glances over from the driver's seat. "'Never sleep with a
woman whose problems are worse than yours'?"

"Right. And wasn't there one about 'Never take advice from
a drunken bartender'?"

"Sober bartender."

"I think it was drunken."

We argue the point for the next thirty miles, since the success of our day depends on it. Last night before dinner as we
sipped some beers, our friendly bartender (steady of hand, glassy
of eye) had raved on and on about what a sleeper the Bechler
was, down in the park's southwest corner. Hard to get to, guaranteed solitude, *big* fish. Sounded most interesting to us—but
was he drunk or sober?

To get to this part of the park you have to drive through Ashton, Idaho, a town I disliked on first sight. Industrial potato fields

that roll quite literally to Yellowstone's very trees—and would certainly go further if it was up to the powers that rule Ashton, right on across the entire park. This is not just an idle worry; back in the 1930s there was a plan boosted locally to build a dam across the Falls River (into which the Bechler flows), creating a huge reservoir over what is in many respects the loneliest, most beautiful corner of the entire park.

There's no entrance gate here, no highway, no tourists, no elk jams. You park at the ranger station (an old blockhouse from the days when the U.S. Army had charge of the park), check in with the ranger if she's about, and start off on a level trail through high, well-spaced pines. It's about a two-hour hike to the Bechler. The trees abruptly end and you come out into an enormous and very flat meadow, decorated on the southeast by the unmistakable verticality of the Tetons, to the north by the closer, shaggier escarpment of the Madison plateau. Beautiful—and yet where in all this was the actual river? It flows in a deep, hidden trench, and since the hiking trail bisects the meadow's center, it's hard knowing whether to go left or go right.

Right—and after a soggy hike through flooded grass it's there: the purest, clearest water I've ever seen (or not seen), so we have to stare at the pebbles on the bottom for a long time before convincing ourselves that they are indeed covered by a flowing liquid, though to call this "water" is to give it more definition and substantiality than, on that first glance, it seems to have.

As we stand there stringing up our rods the wind picks up, strong enough, cold enough, that we plunge down the bank to escape. A little better down here, with the bluff at our backs, but still tricky to cast in, and we have to do it between gusts, loading up quickly and slinging the line out sidearm. But the nice thing about the wind is that it's blowing grasshoppers into the river; not the clouds you find here when the season is at its peak, but enough that the trout are looking *up*. Ray, using an orange-bottomed imitation, catches a rainbow of nearly twenty-five inches that leads him an enormous way down the river; on his way back, still panting from the chase, his face radiant, wind-burned, and happy, he spots another, even bigger trout finning under the overhung bank, and smoothly picks it off. Both of these are hooked, played, and landed on the same 6X tippet, which is to say on pure gossamer skill.

If the Bechler is Ray's finest hour, it turns out to be my poorest. I'm fishing badly, letting the wind bother me, pressing, and for the first time in my fishing life I learn what it's like to experience an overwhelming envy, so it's all I can do to clench my teeth, grunt out a perfunctory "Hey, *nice* fish."

What's going on? I'm shivering in the cold, missing strikes (and what strikes—geysers exploding out of the river when you least expect them), there are big fish about, my back is killing me, and I've come such a long way. All these combine, so the thought of being skunked, a real possibility at this stage, brings me to the point of tears.

We break for lunch on a sandbar where the bank dips away to give us a perfectly framed view of the Tetons. I let the mountains calm me down, do much better in the afternoon, even though the wind only increases. There's nothing like a fish to restore perspective, and what fish these rainbows are, possessing a mature and self-confident wildness, not the furtive, withered kind of wildness trout often display back East. My best fish is just short of twenty inches, thicker than the proverbial football. I miss another, even bigger, but this time I can afford to laugh, as my grasshopper imitation, at the apogee of the explosion, does a slow-motion somersault in midair, lands downstream on its back, and—another trout spotting it—is immediately sent skyward again on the crest of another geyser.

River Six: Boundary Creek. Bushed but happy, we head home about four in order to beat the dark. The cold has deepened, so that's another factor—this is a notoriously bad place for late-summer snowstorms. Boundary Creek is a smaller version of the Bechler flowing out of the forest; where the trail crosses it on a *very* flexible bridge some trout are rising, so we stop and make a few what-the-hell casts. I'm pretty exhausted by this stage, so I let Ray do most of the fishing while I lie there staring out at the enormous meadow, trying to get a deep and lasting impression to bring away with me home—and *click,* I think I have it. Meadow, sunshine, river, fish, Tetons, forest, llamas.

Llamas? Three of them in line, their arrogant, handsome heads snapping slowly back and forth as they glide effortlessly through the marshy ooze. They're led by a happy-looking llama keeper, his head swathed in a red bandanna, and behind come the hikers whose packs the beasts are carrying. There's a campsite a bit further up the creek; the llamas make for it instinctively, circle around the old campfire, crap in unison, collapse knees-first on the grass, and immediately go to sleep.

"Sober," Ray says, wading back out. "The bartender, that is."

"You think so? Anyway, what difference does it make? The man's a genius. We'll go back tonight and buy him three of anything he wants."

River Seven: The Gibbon. Wiped out from the effort of fishing the Bechler, feeling a heavy sense of anticlimax, we're capable of only something modest today and the Gibbon fits the bill. It's one of those friendly riffle-and-pool streams that stays conveniently close to the road; it's longer than you would think judging by its breadth, and extends halfway across the park's middle. Above the falls it's ornamented with paint pots, plate-sized hot springs bubbling away in the shallows, so it's a beautiful combination of classic trout water and world-class exotica, the true Yellowstone mix.

The trout are small and tricky. You can get fifty strikes in fifty yards, and end up hooking only two or three, so fast do they reject a fly. But who cares! We're out to relax and get a feel for this part of the park, and the fish, at least today, are almost an afterthought.

The Madison-Norris corridor was one of the hardest hit spots in the 1988 fires, and blackened trees are everywhere. And while there's new growth prying its way up from the crusty earth (the most delicate curls of a very soft green that you can't look at without wanting to stroke), the dominant note, at least in the blackest groves, is still that of holocaust, a sudden and brutal death.

It's afternoon before the sun bakes the gloominess out of our muscles. We quit early and head back toward town, stopping only long enough to do some sightseeing along the famous park stretch of the Madison known as Seven Mile Run. ("Choice and challenging," one guidebook calls this; "the trout are more elusive and difficult here than anywhere else on the entire river.") Sightseeing, but the wide curve with its fascines of fallen timber, the weed-slicked bottom, and the protective boulders are all so trouty and promising there's no resisting, even in our exhaustion. I catch a decent brown out in the deep current as far as I can cast; it's like a free sample of goodies we'd have to pay dearly for if we really want them, and in the end we decide we've waded out far enough.

On our way back to the car we stop and take a look at the famous Grasshopper Bank on the opposite shore. I'm not impressed—it reminds me of the kind of overly manicured lawn you see in front of corporate headquarters buildings—but that changes in a hurry when a huge trout leaps out of the river and cannonballs back in. Trout will do this to you of course. Wait until the precise moment you've taken down your rod and peeled off your waders, then *boom*—the old cannonball-in-the-water trick. It must keep them smiling for weeks on end.

River Eight: Slough Creek. Little customs and habits are quick to form, even on a fishing trip, and one of the nicest we've fallen into is strolling over after breakfast to Craig Mathews's fly shop. Craig is easily the most famous fly fisherman in these parts, something of a national celebrity for that matter, and why not, since what the man doesn't know about Yellowstone flies and fishing is not worth knowing.

We have some mutual friends. Between this and the instant rapport established between him and Ray, he's taken the time to listen to us, learn what we're after, then gotten us started with what always turns out to be infallible advice.

I say something about fishing Grebe Lake, just for the sake of its grayling—a fish I've never seen, much less captured.

"Oh, you'll catch one all right," Craig says, looking up from the counter where he's just spread some freshly dyed capes. "Small guys, no bigger than my finger. If *I* were fishing today"— and here a note of wistfulness creeps in; even Craig Mathews can't fish every time he wants—"I'd try Slough Creek. Here, take some of these. Mackerel Drake Emergers. You'll slaughter them."

When the Oracle suggests something, you take that suggestion. He follows us outside, goes over the directions once again. "You'll come to the first meadow and see plenty of fish, but keep on walking until you come to the second meadow. Fish there."

You'll see fish but keep on walking—it goes on the table of our trip's ten commandments, and we keep repeating it over and over again all during the long drive across the park.

A great drive. This is the first time I've ever been to the eastern side of the park, driven up the divide near Mount Washburn, seen the view of the Absarokas and the caldera of which they form the distant rim—seen this, then crested the height of land and dropped down the switchbacks to the Yellowstone near Tower Junction, where the landscape goes from thick lodgepole pine forest to those wide and rolling Rocky Mountain plains.

We park just above the Slough Creek campground, note with interest the yellow bear warnings posted on the trail register (definitely shredded—clawed?), then cram our waders into our rucksacks, start out. The hike isn't bad, not after the first steep section, and the trail is a wide one that suggests a well-worn pilgrim's way.

"Here's the meadow," Ray says, where the trees end and the ledges give way.

I stare down into the long slow curve of water that eats into our bank. There's a cutthroat holding in the current, wearing that serious, somber pout fish have when they're resting. I point toward a bigger one, and the shadow cast by my arm is enough to make both quicktail it upstream.

"You'll see some fish—"

"But keep on walking!"

We pass the ranger cabin, resist the urge to cut across the meadow toward those sinuous and sexy Slough Creek curves, stay to the right on the high, flinty trail. Have I said anything yet about the scenery? Where the next grade levels off we take a break near a park-like grove of trees, stare toward the horizon and the snowcapped mountains that rise sharp across the horizon—Granite Peak and its neighbors, the highest summits in Montana, raising the level of the scenery one notch more.

It's another hour to the second meadow. We know we're getting closer when we start encountering some second-meadow kind of guys on their way back down the trail. Young, athletic, looking more like climbers than fly fishermen, with pack rods in the loops where ice axes usually go, they're in too much of a hurry to chat, though we mange to elicit the information that all of them have caught fish.

And yes, the fishing *is* good once we arrive. What's surprising is that we get the entire river to ourselves, or at least the part we pick out. It's downstream of the trail junction—a wide slow pool where the river hooks right before dropping over a shallow ledge, with a terrace of pebbles we can relax on and look things over.

In a fit of madness we start off fishing attractors, but it's obvious the fish aren't interested. What they are interested in are those Drake Emergers we have courtesy of Mr. Mathews. Ray, as usual, catches the first fish—a beautiful copper-dark trout of nearly nineteen inches, with a pronounced yellow shading through the flanks to go along with that characteristic coral flashing on the gills. I hook one a few minutes later, but it takes two of three before I learn to control that first hard, double shake of the head. Pretty soon we've established a regular rhythm. Ray drifts an emerger at the head of the pool, hooks a trout on the rise, gets it under control, leads it through shallow water to the terrace and down the miniature falls while I step in and do exactly the same thing, beaching my fish downstream just about the time Ray has waded back around me to hook his next one.

A lot of cutthroat bashing goes on out West. Some fly fishers claim they're stupid and boring, but what they really are is patient and smart. It's hard to *spook* a cut, true, but it can also be extremely hard to *fool* one, so it's a perfect combination: a fish you get a lot of chances at, but one that's extraordinarily fussy (brook trout back East are exactly the opposite: shy to approach, easy to fool). Matching the hatch is the only option on Slough; it's clear that without Craig's flies we would have been skunked. Even later, when they switch over to size 18 *Baetis*, we're ready for them; one of us or the other is playing a fish the entire time we're there.

A long and perfect afternoon. We might be there yet if it wasn't for the thunderstorms that came up late in the day. With all those mountains and ridges, their tricky acoustics, it's hard to judge when it's time to take cover in the trees. We wait out the worst of these storms under some pines, right in the middle of what's apparently a favorite grizzly lair, judging by the whitened mounds of turds, the sun-bleached pile of half-gnarled bones. Talk about your frissons! Lightning bolts flaring down at your forehead, grizzly poop underneath your butt! What a remarkable country this is!

River Nine: The Gallatin. We've become advice junkies, and when we can't borrow or beg some, we're not above stealing our daily fix. This morning what we basically do is overhear a conversation in the next booth—a couple of guide types, judging by the gravel guards wedged around their ankles, the Polaroids tucked in at their throats. What they're talking about is the Gallatin—how crowded it is in its lower reaches, but how no one bothers fishing the meadow portion where it leaves the highway and climbs toward the mountains. There aren't any trout for the first mile of this stretch—no one knew why—but then they appeared again, and you had to keep hiking in order to locate this spot.

Was this a deliberate piece of misinformation planted to put two uppity dudes in their place? We hike a mile and then some without any sight of fish, this despite the fact that the Gallatin is perfectly clear here, and with the banks so high it would be easy to spot anything swimming about.

"Maybe we haven't gone a mile?" Ray says, mopping off his face with his hat.

I finally do spot a brown, a nice one, but he's not interested in my hopper. By this time we're halfway up the valley, hungry, hot, and tired. The only redeeming virtue is the wildlife—mule deer, a coyote, some eagles, and an elk. We also have a good conversation with a park ranger on horseback, on his way into the backcountry for a two-week patrol. Sharing a soda, he tells us some good stories about elk poachers—how smart the smart ones are, how stupid the remainder.

We've fished together a long time, Ray and I—it only takes a glance for each of us to know the other wants to turn back. Once to the car we revive enough to spend the afternoon on the Madison. The drift boats have already floated through, so we pretty much have it to ourselves except for an osprey. We're a lot more relaxed this time, and as a result do well. A whitefish tricks me into thinking it's a brown, and after hollering Ray over to net it I feel pretty sheepish at what emerges. A few minutes later, hooking what I think is another huge whitefish, I play it casually, afraid to get my hopes up, then am surprised—and even more sheepish—to find it's a brown trout of nearly three pounds.

River Ten: The Gardner. We're here for several reasons. We haven't seen the Mammoth Hot Springs part of the park, it's on our way back to Bozeman, and we have time for one last stream before driving back to the airport. Then too, this is by way of homage to the late Charles F. Brooks. We bought his *Fishing Yellowstone Waters* before we came out here, used it to plan our trip, and have found it a reliable and entertaining source of information all the way around the circuit. "Let's see what Charlie says" is another of our refrains. Stream-smart, literate, someone who never lost sight of the ambient beauty, he must have been a fine man to fish with.

Here's what he says about the Gardner:

> The five miles or so of stream in the Mammoth area are very pleasant miles to fish. There is just enough difficulty getting into and out of the stream and in fishing it to deter the casual. It is a prolific piece of water *for the proficient fly fisher.* The fish are larger than farther up, and there are now and then run-up fish from the Yellowstone. You must know what you are about to do well in the lower Gardner.

It's all true. The day is a hot one, and this side of the park is more arid than anything we've seen so far, so the hike down to the river, or at least the prospect of hiking back up again, seems like a particularly grueling ordeal. But what the hell—it's our last day, and when we finish we can cool off with some beers.

Charles is right about those run-up fish. We see some on the other side of the river, dark, torpedo-like shapes perfectly aligned with one another as they face the heavy current, for all the world like cathode figures in a video game waiting for quarters to be dropped in before moving. With trees behind us and a steep bank, they're impossible to reach. Further upstream we find the fish wary, but catchable; one of these turns out to be a brook trout, a little guy who's probably run down the river from one of the beautifully named creeks that make up its headwaters, Fawn, Indian, Panther, or Obsidian. The views here are high, wide, and handsome, though you're looking *up* at them, not out or down, and this makes us feel good insignificant and good small. Three mountain sheep are playing on the cliffs—not a common sighting, even in Yellowstone.

Nothing major to report here, but a taste of what canyon fishing is all about, and the pleasant, relaxed kind of finale we're after. Weighted down by some extra juice cartons, my vest rips in half, dropping fly boxes into the river that Ray, wading below me, gracefully scoops up. I'm saddened; on a long trip you come to live in your vest, cramming it with sandwiches, rain gear, aspirin, candy bars, and sodas, let alone flies and tackle, so it becomes something much more essential and organic than mere fabric—it's as if a well-worn but dearly loved part of my flesh, tiring of life, has shredded away.

Time for that beer. We find a bar in Gardiner that's long, dark, and empty—the green on the pool table alone is enough to cool us off. We knock back a quick one, then take our time with the refill, talking about our trip, letting it start to settle, concerned that we do this just right. We agree that our survey, big-gulp kind of approach has worked well, giving us both the kind of wide overview that makes sense for a first trip, and a much more detailed, intimate kind of hands-on experience as well. Reading everything we could find, asking everyone questions, experimenting, exploring, we've learned quite a bit, will be much better prepared next time we come out here—a trip that's already entered its planning stage by the time that second beer goes down.

And it's a funny thing. Even sitting in that deserted bar with those beers, our muscles sore from all the hiking and wading, the rivers seem to flow into one, so the Madison in our memory becomes just a wider portion of Nez Percé Creek, the Bechler just another meadow up from the Firehole, whose headwaters drop into the Gallatin, the mouth of which forms the Gardner, with no dividing line at all, not even the narrow enough one that barely separates them in reality. I think of Aldo Leopold and how he tried to find the appropriate phrase to sum up the interconnectedness of the living world, the biotic stream, and how he came up with the perfect one: *the Round River*. Yellowstone's rivers, wildlife, forest, meadows, lakes, and ponds flow into one another and are one, that's the moral; nowhere else in the world would it have been possible for us to navigate so much riverine beauty in so short a time.

There's some sadness here, the kind that comes when a good fishing trip is finished, but more than that, too. The kind that comes to an aging athlete who knows between one game and the next that the glory days are over, and while he will play on for a few more years yet, it will never be at the same intense level. Hiking to all those streams, forcing our way up rapids, taking some spills, letting the rocks knock us around, the hot press of the sun, the prying leverage of that wind. I know, sitting there in that dark cowboy bar, that I'll never be capable of such a prolonged physical effort again—know, too, that it's all right to be sad with this, since it's another part of the Round River, and I'd be a fool to wish myself free of its current.

What we need is a line to go out on, and Ray pulls one from the silence, raising his glass with the last of the beer. "You'll see fish," he says, squinting, "but keep on walking."

I nod, laugh, tilt my own glass back for its last quarter inch of foam. "You might not think they're there, but—"

We finish in unison. "They're there!"

River Eleven: The Lamar. A line to go out on—and yet there is one last river in our trip, a sunset to talk about, the kind that should by rights end any good Western. On our next-to-last night Ray stays in town to make some phone calls while I drive over to the Lamar just upstream of its canyon. While the water itself is invisible, the river's route through the valley is marked plain enough by the declination and fold of the banks, and so it's no problem at all to walk through the sagebrush and boulders until I find a likely looking pool. There's a rainbow waiting between two rocks—he jumps when I hook him and jumps again just for fun. So close have I timed things that by the time I land him it's dark enough I have to head back to the car.

From where I'm parked the land rolls toward the west like a very wide inclined plane, up which a transparent force is rolling itself toward the mountains that rise above the intersecting furrow of the Yellowstone two miles away. Even the mountains, steep as they are, seem only a higher, more rugged version of this ramp, so they too are helping boost this invisible something into the sky. Above the mountains, as I stare, this force manifests itself in layer upon layer of clouds, flat on the lenticular edges, billowy in their softer centers, the mass expanding upward and outward as I watch. There's hardly any variation in color from one superimposed layer to the next, and yet by the time the layers end they have gone from a base of stony gray to a ceiling that's a dramatic and vivid crimson—all this done in such gradual increments it's impossible to point to any one place on the horizon and say *there,* the color's different.

The most beautiful sunset I've ever seen? It ranks right up there. Somewhere behind the ridges the sun is just high enough to take the color and give it a name, a quality, and definition: *loneliness.* It's loneliness I'm watching, not the sad kind we feel ourselves, but the kind that has shadings of great pity and acceptance—what the land might feel for us if it bothered noticing our presence at all. It seems the whole wide untouched Yellowstone landscape is scrolling itself toward the heavens to pronounce a judgment, some final word, and then—and this was a very poignant thing to watch—the color suddenly leaves it, from bottom layer to top, and with it all the difficult meaning, so for one last moment it's the empty land itself that is mirrored there in the sky, before man could color and tame it with his own longing . . . and finally in a last flash of something that isn't quite orange, the sky rolls over into blackness, the wind comes up off the river, my shoulders start shaking, and it's time to go home.

August 25

THE YELLOWSTONE is not only the most prolific trout river in North America but also the most intimidating, especially inside the national park. Above Yellowstone Lake on the Thorofare Plateau the wading isn't bad, *if* you can get there; it's a long hike in, from whatever direction, and the country is known for its quicksand and grizzlies. Just downstream of the lake is the notorious Fishing Bridge, where the trout butchers used to do their thing, but fishing is no longer permitted there, and with the river flowing at full breadth from one of the largest lakes in the country it wouldn't be any place to wade. The water in Hayden Valley is approachable and choice, but fishing isn't permitted there either, even though it's alive with feeding trout. Further downstream are the famous falls, among the highest on the continent; below these is a thousand-foot-deep canyon with precipitous walls of smooth and friable rock. Even at Tower Junction, where the river re-emerges, the water flows past at warp speed, and this only gets worse further downstream in the hard to get to, impossible to wade section known as Black Canyon.

If you do manage to find a place to fish you can sense all this wild and lusty exuberance working on you as you step into the water—the weight of Yellowstone Lake upstream, the giddiness of the falls just below. This is the longest untamed river in the lower forty-eight states, and the water, its very molecules, seem powered by this freedom, so they bear down on you with double the weight and energy of normal H_2O. This is water, cold water, that has been here a lot longer than man has and will be here rushing and tumbling and foaming downstream long after he is gone—and it's not above taking a sacrificial victim with it now and then to demonstrate this principle.

Between rapids and canyons and falls and regulations, there are very few stretches of the Yellowstone you can wade safely, let alone comfortably. One of these is called Buffalo Ford—*the* Buffalo Ford, famous for its cutthroats, pictured in all the magazines, the very epicenter of fly fishing's remarkable boom, and on a typical summer's day the most heavily fished pool in the world.

Not a place for the loner, the shy one, the fastidious. And yet on a warm and sunny late-August morning this was exactly who waded through the bright skipping water on its edge, stopped to look things over, stood rocking back and forth in his wading brogues, counting the number of fishermen he could see in the river, vowing that when he reached fifty he would turn around again and go back to his car. Something of an old hand now in this part of the world, a man who was taking a break from the family on what was otherwise a family trip all the way, he had deliberately avoided the Yellowstone on his two previous trips out West, scared off not only by the power of the water, but the power of that mob.

How many? Two fishermen just to the right of him, gearing up. Another straight ahead on the edge of an island, tight to a fish. A man and woman holding onto each other for balance, the current piling up in a golden *W* around their waists. Three scattered in the shallower water on the far and distant shore, one casting, one wading, one pointing a camera at the stolid echelon of buffalo grazing on the bank.

Seven fly fishers, not counting himself. Seven in a river that could swallow dozens and hardly show the strain. Whether because it was late August and the crowds had gone home, or because of some favorable, impossible-to-predict eddy in the current that compelled people to fish here, the fisherman had come on a day when for all intents and purposes he had the Yellowstone River to himself.

So, no excuses. He checked to see his wader belt was fastened, shuffled his boots against the pebbles on the bottom to clear them of weed, then slanted his way into the current, taking a line that would bring him above the island and into the slower water on the far side. Not hard wading, but not easy either—the Yellowstone may be fordable on four legs here, but two legs is difficult. Between the fast current, the bottom that alternates between pebbles and clay, the kind of moral vulnerability you feel when out in any big river alone, the fisherman was more than a little relieved when the bottom started shelving upward again, the pebbles came back, the water left off pushing solid on his waist and took to kicking broken on his shins.

Safe. He paused, feeling a certain triumph, then turned, startled, at a loud whuffing sound that was even deeper than the river's whoosh. Buffalo, another long file, coming into the river just behind him. They didn't seem to do this intentionally, with premeditation; they were grazing at the top of the bank, one or two stepped over, and before they understood what was happening the whole herd was caught up in a mindless inertia that carried them at a half-gallop into the river, where they stood snorting, coughing, and grunting, wondering why they were even there.

There was no exaggerating the fun of watching them. America is so full of place-names that no longer make sense—Trout Lake, with no trout in them; Cougar Canyons with no cougar—that it was good to be standing in a place that was literally being rechristened *Buffalo Ford* as he watched.

Where the bank jutted out into the river was another fly fisher, a woman this time. At this sport for well over thirty years, he'd only seen a woman fishing by herself three or four times, all on this trip, so it was clear the demographics were changing and changing rapidly. This particular woman was no beginner; she cast far and she cast fast, with nothing wasted in her motion. Stocky, she moved through the water with great delicacy and confidence, a disciplined skater in full command. With the sun behind her, the fly line decorating the sky overhead, the wind tossing back her hair, she managed in that beautiful landscape to take on a great deal of beauty herself; an old-fashioned poetical mind might have seen her as the very spirit of the river, and not be far wrong.

A few pleasantries—*How's the fishing? Fine! Three cuts!*—and then he was on his way again, climbing up onto the bank and taking off through the woods upstream. This was easier than forcing his way through the current, but not all that much easier, since blowdown pines were everywhere, and it was impossible to hike in a straight line.

Where to start? One of the conceptual tricks in fishing a big river is to try to break it up into smaller, more comprehensible channels within the expanse, not be overawed. This is hard to do on the Yellowstone—it sweeps impetuously along, with no thought for a fisherman's convenience—but not impossible. A hundred yards more of walking and the steep bank crumbled away, widening the river no more than eleven or twelve feet, and yet by this expansion making it lose several vital gallons per second of force. Some pines had fallen with the bank, and their roots were still strong enough to hold the trunks perpendicular to the current, breaking it up even more.

It wasn't long before he discovered the limits of this eddy; in tight by the bank all was fine, but eight or nine steps out it was a different story. The current was even faster and harder than it appeared from shore, so there was no going deeper than his hips without being bowled over. The bottom was tricky, too; a coating of pebbles and gravel gave good purchase, but mixed in were elliptical patches where the current had washed the gravel away, exposing the bone-white clay underneath—and to step onto one of these clay patches meant a fast ride down toward Yellowstone Falls.

Things finally settled with his feet, he began looking about for trout. They were there all right—cutthroats of seventeen and eighteen inches right in front of him, though it took a few minutes before his eyes got accustomed enough to the water's glare to penetrate it, see beneath. Back in New England, where he did most of his fishing, you could go all summer without sight-fishing to a trout, so the experience was a new one to him and exhilarating. He was fishing an attractor pattern just attractive enough to make the trout, as it floated downstream, raise their heads a fraction of an inch, quiver in interest, then—the fraud becoming apparent—relax again in boredom and sink back to their original, tail-slightly-below-head position. The same happened when he fished a nymph, though this time they were interested enough to move laterally in the current to appraise it from the side, even bluff it with a little charge, before lapsing into that same irrefutable indifference.

He'd always heard these Buffalo Ford cutthroats were picky, and it gave him an odd satisfaction to learn the stereotype was true—it was like learning that all Parisians are indeed rude. It took three hours of hard work before he caught one. Tired of fishing upstream, he climbed back out onto the bank, switched to a sink-tip line, took a long detour inland, then balanced his way out along one of the fallen trees and roll cast a weighted stonefly into the current to let it swing down.

A fish was on it right away, an important fish. The fisherman was always somewhat casual in playing trout, but there was often one during a trip that he simply *had* to land, and this was one of those—the fate of the day was resting upon this. And he did catch it, but not without making a spectacle of himself. The fish continued upstream after fastening, but then balked at too much pressure and made an abrupt U-turn, not only stripping out line to the backing, but pulling the reel off the rod, so the fisherman had to grab for it in the current, hold it in his hand, and start down the shallows in pursuit—right onto one of those treacherous clay patches. When he got up again—when with some frantic screwing he got his reel reattached—the trout was still on, though an enormous distance downstream. His fall on the clay had muddied up the river, so it seemed the trout was fleeing the milky gray cloud as much as it was the pressure of the line, and by the time he caught up with it, landed it, photographed it, let it go, he was soaked through with river, sweat, and clay, and yet happy past all description.

Clumsy, but no fool, he'd packed along some extra clothes for just such an eventuality. Dry, somewhat composed, feeling stubborn, he hooked another cutthroat from exactly the same position, walked over to the bank, sat down on a rock, and played it in comfort, refusing to engage in any more shenanigans.

He ate lunch on top of the bank in what sundial-like shade a lodgepole pine casts. A nap would have been nice, but he got caught up in watching the pelicans, a bird he had always associated with Florida, not Wyoming. Squadrons of them flew down from Yellowstone Lake, much more graceful than the comic image you get from cartoons. Their whiteness, their airiness, did a lot to cool him off.

When he got his fill of these, there were buffalo, a few of them anyway. They seemed bewildered by the fallen timber, confused that there shouldn't be an easy way down to the river; with a few bothered snorts they wheeled around again and headed back to the ford that bore their name.

The fishing was better in the afternoon—rising trout now, coming up to those tiny *Baetis* that are everywhere in a Yellowstone August. This was sight-fishing again, at least toward the end of the rise, when a yellow-brown verticality would appear underneath the fly and slowly continue upward through the surface film, remaining there for a long and very visible moment before looping back down again. Hooked upstream, these fish were easier to land, and after three or four the fisherman decided there was nothing more to ask of the day. His total wasn't high, and yet the point had been made: yes, the Yellowstone was indeed the most prolific trout river in America, the breadth of it, the very substance of the water, alive with the presence of wild and beautiful fish.

He was taking down his rod on top of the bank when an invisible and yet very real force (strong enough to be felt even with the competition of the river) made him turn around. Where the bank dipped away to let a wet spot seep into the river was what he thought at first was a coyote. A second later it saw him and stopped; it was very obviously trying to decide whether to continue past him or change direction and retreat back into the woods.

The fisherman started to reach into his vest for his camera, then thought better of it. Coyotes were nothing new. Coyotes— why, they had coyotes right at home, trotting across their meadow in the course of their daily rounds. No, he wasn't going to waste film on a mere coyote.

Like a hungry and very gaunt German shepherd—that's how he described coyotes to friends who had never seen one. But then something in the animal's posture changed, some slight squaring readjustment in the way it was standing, and he realized it wasn't a gaunt German shepherd at all, but an extraordinarily healthy German shepherd, one with height and muscle, a princely attitude, and all the self-confidence in the world . . . that it wasn't a coyote at all, but the cherished object of a careful reintroduction campaign, a hero all the media was going nuts over, the subject of all those campfire talks by the rangers: a live and very real wolf.

A wolf, not ten yards away. There was no fear in this encounter, on either side. The fisherman looked at the wolf, childishly pleased that after hearing about them for so long he should actually be face to face with one; the wolf, for his part, stared into the man's expression with an alert kind of interest in which something was reciprocated, though it was impossible to say exactly what. Something mammalian at any rate; the wolf's alertness wasn't that different than the alertness of the trout, and yet that second, deeper something was much different, a consanguine kind of recognition nothing cold-blooded could ever manage.

There's no end to this encounter, not in dramatic terms. The lone wolf turned and walked unhurriedly along the riverbank; the lone fisherman turned and did the same in the opposite direction. When he entered the timber he stopped and looked back—but there they parted company, for that wolf, finding nothing remarkable in the encounter, trotted away without glancing back over his shoulder at all.

Family Trout

THE CONVENTIONAL WISDOM is that anyone who tries to combine a serious fly-fishing trip with a traditional family vacation is asking for trouble. The two simply don't mix—never have, never will. A fly fisher, reduced to essentials, is someone who's willing to travel many hundreds of miles in order to feel a tug on the end of a thin piece of line, often finding that this simple enough sensation brings with it various spiritual benefits. Of course not everyone in the family might have the same kind of yearning—there are tugs exerted by tourist attractions and art galleries, Indian reservations and historical sites, water slides and hiking trails—and so another kind of tug is created, a competitive, intramural one, the kind that when it comes to deciding how to spend the day can quite literally tear a family apart.

And yet it's so tempting—the idea of taking the family to a place where the fishing is good! The fly fisher arranges things so he has two or three days to himself, vows to be good the rest of the time, agrees the spouse can have a corresponding amount of time to do what she wants, tells himself it will be a terrific bonding experience with the kids. All this sounds great, the deposit is mailed, airline tickets reserved, junior fishing outfits purchased. So perfect are the arrangements that the fly fisher then makes a fatal mistake—he actually follows through on it—and what seems so doable in January turns out to be a fiasco in July.

For the problems are not only real, but nearly inescapable. Fly fishing is not much fun to watch if you're nine and Dad (or Mom) is the one doing it; nine is usually too young to master the intricate rhythm of casting, summon up the requisite patience; nine, especially out West, is too young to go wandering off by yourself along a precipitous and fast-moving river. Nine, in other words, is no fun at all. Of course, forty-five can be difficult too. Here you are, in a situation where by rights you should be at your most demanding and selfish as regards *your* fun, at the very same instant your family is the most selfish and demanding about *their* fun. Both parties are right, absolutely right, and yet as anyone who's been at this game for a while knows, the arguments where both parties are right often turn out to be the most damaging, lasting, and bitter.

But it can work. With luck, with a willingness to compromise, with some imagination, the right locale, combining a family vacation with a serious fly-fishing trip can work extraordinarily well, and I would like to offer my own family as the happy, living proof. Our trip to Yellowstone was a success from start to finish, in fly-fishing terms and family-vacation terms both, and yet even while we basked in the miracle of this we didn't fully realize *how* successful until the very last moment of our very last day.

If there is one place on earth where the family versus fly-fishing trick can be pulled off, it's Yellowstone. Big as the park is, it's still relatively compact, at least in the way it combines trout places and kid places. It's perfectly possible to start the day out on a trout river, be back at the lodge in time to have breakfast with the family, go hiking all day without seeing another person, do a waterfall or scenic loop on the way back, then—if you've the energy—go out again after dinner and do some more fishing while the family turns in.

This became the pattern of our days, right from the start. Driving down from the airport in Bozeman, we stopped in Livingston to stock up on picnic supplies, including flies at Dan Bailey's, where the women fly tyers working by their window made a big fuss over Matthew, age five, and gave him some peacock herl as a souvenir. An hour later the kids were running up the boardwalk along Mammoth Hot Springs, marveling not only at the way the earth literally turns itself inside out, but how the elk, even on a hot August day, like to lie in the hottest, steamiest spots. Then it was time to check into our simple cabin at Roosevelt Lodge; after dinner (chicken-fried steak with all the corn muffins we could handle), it was over to the nearby Lamar, where Dad caught trout while the rest of the family had a great time exploring the banks, climbing over the boulders, taking pictures of the buffalo, cheering Dad on.

This by way of warm-up. Next morning the trip got fully in gear with a hike to a remote lake only a few hundred yards back from the east rim of the Grand Canyon of the Yellowstone. We've found over the years that kids hike best when there's a real magnet or attraction at the end, and by magnet I mean a fire tower, a cliff, or a pond. Of these, a pond works best; mountain summits, alluring enough to adults, are a bit too abstract to motivate a young child, but a *pond,* the aura of brightness it carries, the prospect of coolness, is enough to make even a reluctant hiker keep going.

We parked in the huge empty lot near the Lower Falls, hitched up our rucksacks, tied and retied all bootlaces, stuck a pack rod in Dad's pack, started out. The trail hugs the canyon's rim for the first mile, and we kept stopping to go gingerly over and peer down. Both kids remained very much in character as they did this. Erin, tall, curious, a determined thinker, took in the depth, the sheerness, the cataract of foaming whiteness an incredible distance down below, and did a little inward double-clutch with her chin—*whoa,* her expression plainly said, *what have we here?* Matthew, four years younger at five, reacted like his mother did—this great and glorious canyon made him giggle, set his glasses to jiggling on his nose, and he looked over at us, wanting us to share his fun.

It was an hour's hike to the lake—two lakes actually, one set like a transparent soup bowl inside a golden meadow that perfectly doubled it; the other smaller, cup-sized, trickling into the larger via a soft little creek. Trout were rising the moment we arrived, and I started right in on them. Celeste and Erin took their hiking boots off, waded in the cool shallows; Matthew took his boots off, too, then his pants, then his shirt, then, stripped to essentials, went after the salamanders as assiduously as he did at home.

Something for all of us here. After trying every fly I'd brought along, I found a small black nymph that took them on just about every cast—little rainbows, beautiful rainbows, waiting just beyond the fringe of weeds. I got Matthew to leave off the amphibians long enough to catch one, then it was Erin's turn, then Celeste's. When the sun got stronger the women went back under the trees for a nap, but Matthew and I kept at it, taking turns with the sunscreen, alternating slugs from the canteen, working our way around the edge of the pond to the narrow inlet where the bottom was sandy and we could wade a long way out.

Hiking back to the car, as high and happy as the canyon was deep and dark, the kids learned something else about the Yellowstone experience. The parking lot that had been empty when we started was now overflowing with tour buses and cars; the ramps and decks where you walk out to see the falls had long lines of tourists waiting their chance to snap a picture, and a great deal of shoving was going on as people tried to get at the rail.

"This is nutso!" Celeste yelled—the mob scene suggested more noise than it was actually producing.

"Bazookas!" Erin said, upping the ante.

"Crazy," I nodded. Then, "Hey, let's get a picture!"

Seeing a gap, the four of us wedged our way against the wooden rail with the white-green plunge of Lower Falls at our backs. A young hiker stood there seemingly as confused and horrified at the crowds as we were, and Celeste instantly picked him out as the one to ask.

"Sure," he said, with a big grin. Celeste handed him the camera, gave him quick instructions, stepped back. "This will be your Christmas card," he said, squinting—and he called it right. The picture came out perfect, the four of us posed there like we have the falls all to ourselves—me wearing yet another of the floppy hats that have accompanied my life like ludicrous banners; Celeste and Erin with matching grins, the bandannas pulling their hair back so their resemblance, so subtle most of the time, is obvious and striking; Matthew tucked in between us, a natural the moment a camera is near, with a forthright and charismatic grin that's enough to upstage even a higher, happier waterfall than Yellowstone's.

All this forms the first piece of advice I have for a fly fisher who has the family along—build the fishing into a hike. The second suggestion is to devote a day to having just the kids catch fish, leaving your own rod back in the car. There's a guide service based at the marina on Yellowstone Lake, small cabin cruisers that go out after cutthroats. We called ahead for reservations and our guide was waiting for us when we arrived. John was his name—a tall man with a Chicago Bulls cap on who coaches junior high basketball in the off-season in a town just outside the park. He smiled at the kids' eagerness, but it seemed a bit forced; late August now, he was getting more than a little burned out from the thousands of cuts he had caught in the course of the summer.

"Maybe we'll get a laker," he said hopefully, as he powered us out into open water.

Lake trout is what he meant, a controversial subject. Some madman had apparently dumped lake trout into the lake, thereby putting at risk the finest wild cutthroat fishery in the world. Who had done it? When? According to John there had been thirty-pound fish caught, and this would indicate the lakers had been in there a lot longer than just two summers. The Fish and Wildlife Service was trying very hard to get a handle on the situation, but they were handicapped by lack of funds; the only way they had been able to afford a simple fish finder for their runabout was when the guides chipped in to buy one for them.

"I wouldn't mind catching one," John said. "Just for the change, I mean."

I could see his point. The cutthroats in Yellowstone Lake are not hard to catch, which was fine by me, since I very much wanted the kids to have some fast and easy action. We headed into the light chop in the lake's center, then, using a distant bluff as his reference point, John got the ultralight spinning gear rigged up, explained to the kids what was required of them, flipped the bails back, let their spinners trail out in the jacuzzi-like bubbles of our wake.

Thirty seconds after the line went out, forty at the most, Matthew had a hit. He sat bolt upright on his bench, started reeling in as if his life depended on it, and a few minutes later John landed his cutthroat, held it by Matt's shoulder for a photo, deftly removed the hook with pliers, and dropped the fish back into the lake (cuts, the big ones, have to be put back here; any laker *has* to be kept, setting up a situation where you can be fined for practicing catch and release). The moment this was accomplished Celeste had a fish on, and then a few minutes later, just when she worried she would be left out of the fun, it was Erin's turn, with the biggest one yet. Not five minutes went by without one of them catching a trout, and when once the gap went to six minutes, John (who was studying his watch) acted disgusted and instantly tried a different spot.

"Slow today," he said, without irony. "Must be those clouds moving in."

Me, I was having a great time, even though I wasn't fishing other than vicariously. Partly this was from thinking about those cutthroat—how amazing it was they would be so close to the surface in such featureless water miles from shore. Partly—and any fisherman will understand this—it was from the comfortable, reassuring sense of propinquity you get just being near any large and healthy congregation of fish. I asked John about going after them with a fly rod; he insisted I come back in July some year, when you can cruise the shallows and take trout after trout right on top.

Most of all, though, I was enjoying being out on Yellowstone Lake for the first time. All through the park you're immersed in a landscape that can feature both an exhilarating sense of expanse and, with those rivers and remote ponds, great watery beauty of much variety, and yet it's only when out in the middle of this enormous lake in a boat, seeing the mountains that ring it, feeling on your face the wind that blows up from the Tetons, absorbing with your legs its swells, that you realize you still have much to learn when it comes to both water and expanse—that what you've seen in the park is only by way of a preliminary to this fluid masterpiece of water, mountain, and sky.

After an hour of this—after the kids had each caught a dozen trout—the storm that had been hovering over the mountains all morning now lashed down in magnificent violence right above our heads. We stuck it out for a few more fish, then the kids made a dive for the cabin (which looked so cozy and kid-sized they'd been eyeing it with interest ever since we came out) while Celeste and I crowded in near John at the wheel for the bouncy ride back in.

By the time we reached the dock the worst of the storm was over; a well-scrubbed sun was already streaming through the pines along shore. We thanked John, wished him well for the coming basketball season. Hope you kill one of those lakers, I told him. He smiled, bashfully, then glanced down at the notebook I only now realized he'd been scribbling in since the moment we docked.

"Two thousand three hundred and forty-six cutthroats," he said, with a perceptible sigh. "Trolling, every last one."

With our joint expeditions having gone so well, it was time for the old I'll-go-fishing-while-you-guys-go-sightseeing gambit, one I've tried before, though with mixed success. The family always has a good time without Dad, which is just the point: I get lonely without them, actually homesick, and often find the fishing can't compete with the fun of watching the kids climb a new mountain or see their very first geyser.

But this time it went well—better than well. I had a good day fishing the Yellowstone, and when I got back to the lodge at night I found the three of them already in the middle of dinner. They waved to me when I came into the dining room, glanced over at each other like conspirators who've agreed on a plan, stifled some giggles, seemed on the point of bursting with what was obviously great and important news.

The story broke upon me the moment I sat down—a collaborative effort told in the rushing kind of multi-part harmony families get so good at over time. This is what happened. After breakfast, according to plan, they had driven to Old Faithful, arriving just after one of its periodic eruptions. Old Faith has slowed down over the years due to earthquakes; for a second Celeste wondered if it was worth waiting the hour or so for the next display.

A half hour passes—the three of them wander over toward Old Faithful Lodge for a snack. Rangers all around. *Lots* of rangers. Men in suits and sunglasses, too, looking edgy. The kind of nondescript crowd that gathers in these situations, as if there are always extras stashed behind the shrubbery ready to jump out when needed. Someone pointing toward the sky—"They're here!" Helicopters appearing over the tree tops, landing in the parking lot in a huge circle made by rangers holding hands. Flashbulbs going off, video cameras, men rushing to get a better position, everyone pointing.

The President descends. As in, the President of these United States. Wife. Daughter. Walking quickly to the elevated terrace forty feet from where Celeste, Matthew, and Erin stand innocently chewing their chocolate chip cookies.

"Wave," Celeste says. Erin waves, shyly. Matthew, shy, not knowing why he has to be, waves, too. President's daughter catches his eye, waves back, shy herself. Shyness National Park.

Camera doesn't work, natch. Names and addresses exchanged with woman next to them, her promising to send picture. President in short sleeves and chinos. President's wife in floppy hat and sundress. President's daughter in jeans. Everyone pointing . . . crowd half-turns . . . Old Faithful blossoms toward the sky.

What an adventure! I'm sorry to have missed it, but not that sorry, since nothing could match the anticipation I saw in their faces when I came into the dining room, the happy eagerness with which the story came bubbling out. It wasn't until dessert that all the ramifications and little details were correctly tucked away; it was only then that Matthew remembered that someone else in the family had been out searching for stories of his own.

"Hey Dad," he said, chomping down on his seventh corn muffin. "Catch any fish?"

The next few days all had trout in them, even if it was only those small, delightful cutthroats you can catch in the tributary streams while your family enjoys a picnic in the lush undergrowth that has sprung up under the fire-blackened trees from the 1988 fires (venerable-looking now, like pillars pitted and smoothed by the forces of time). I slipped away again for a long day on Slough Creek, there were a couple of more hikes, and by our last day there was very little more to ask of our week.

It seemed greedy wanting anything more from Yellowstone, especially when we woke up to find our fine weather had moved out and it was raining heavily. We drove along the Lamar past the ranger station, the clouds hanging collapsed and crumpled on the peaks that line the road, the buffalo standing motionless, the fly fishers looking gloomily out their car windows, the entire life of the park seeming to have come to a sodden dead stop. Not immune to this mood, tired from our week, we made the mistake of driving on to Cooke City to get something to eat. I hated it from the moment we drove in, the very look of the place; it reeked of poachers and gold miners, stream rapers, "locals" who had moved there from California and were now mewing about how by rights it was *their* park. . . . Well, it was that kind of day.

Time to get going. We felt better the second we crossed back into the park, and what's more the sun was starting to come out now, and as Celeste drove westward I stared at our map searching for one last backcountry lake we could hike to before it was time to head home.

The one I picked out was just far enough back in the mountains to deter the casual; only three acres in extent, it was famous for the impressive size of its trout—and always had been. As I read later in a history of the park, the lake had been the scene of the first game bust in Yellowstone's history, when the early rangers had surprised some poachers from Cooke City who were illegally netting out the lake's enormous cutthroats. A few years later, trout were taken out of the pond to use in the park's first hatchery, since it was clear they were of a genetic strain it was worth trying to reproduce.

I didn't know this at the time—for all I knew, the lake was fishless, as so many in Yellowstone are. We parked on the pull-off, got our gear together quickly as befits old hands, then started up the trail through a delightful meadow whose late-summer wildflowers were damp enough to come alive in the sunshine like, to use my son's phrase, wet lollipops hidden in the grass.

The trail met the lake at its timbered outlet. It was a ragged kind of circle, completely open except for the patch of trees on our side, and surrounded by a steep, sandy bank that formed a kind of mezzanine looking down into the ginger-ale–colored (my daughter's simile this time) water. The alpine meadow started on the upslope edge of this bench; every way you looked, staring through the ribbony partings the sun made in the mist, your eyes ran into blue-gray mountains, the highest with snow.

Something else was needed before the scene became perfect—and there it was. Just on the edge of the lake, slightly below a raft of fallen branches: a quick swirl of something that immediately disappeared. A cutthroat? Probably. It's often all we ever see of wildlife, that quick flick of the tail that takes it from our presence, but it was enough to make me appraise the lake differently, notice what I should have noticed sooner: the soft dimpled rings pushed into the surface, not by leftover raindrops, but by rising trout.

By the time we walked around to the open portion of the lake I had my rod up, ready to cast. As usual in these circumstances, the trout were feeding about three yards past my furthest cast, and the bottom was too soft to wade out even one step more. Celeste kept on going where the trail started to curve, then looked back to take my picture. It's on the wall behind me as I write, a calendar shot, me following through on a cast, my left hand caught in a tossing motion as it releases the line, my right shoulder curved into the plane of the cast, my rod pointing horizontally toward a doubled loop of line caught at the very moment of opening—all this framed and decorated by the yellow meadow grass at my waist, the pines in the background, the mountains rising behind a decorative cliché of airy mist.

Classic form—but I couldn't quite reach those trout. Celeste and the kids watched for a few moments, then, obviously giving up on me, continued on around the lake and vanished over a little ridge. About ten minutes later, while I was still fussing and fretting over my impotence regarding the gulpers, Matthew ducked back over the ridge; in his excitement, the frantic way he waved, I thought of a cavalry scout sent to summon reinforcements.

"Over here, Dad! They're over there! Big ones!"

I quickly reeled in. "Don't scare them!" I yelled, but he was already gone.

The first thing I saw as I hurried to catch up was that they were standing well back from the bank, in no danger of scaring them. In no danger of scaring *what* took longer to figure out. Celeste was pointing and Erin was jumping up and down and Matthew was bending forward with the rigid intentness of a pointer, and so excited were all these postures that my first reaction was that a great white shark had somehow gotten loose in the lake.

I wasn't far wrong. It was trout they were staring at, lots of trout, fat cutthroats that were almost twenty inches long. They were swimming around and around the shallows where a narrow inlet stream bubbled in—the kind of frantic behavior you would expect to see in spawning time in early July. But this was late August—what was going on? They were feeding on top, plucking midges from the surface film, and I knew in the first instant of spotting them both what was expected of me and how hard it was going to be to pull this off.

"Catch them!" Celeste commanded.

"The reddish one," Matthew added, making it sound like "radish."

"Rip their lips!" Erin yelled.

The blood lust was spreading, and why not, faced with those beautiful fish we could have reached out and touched with a stick. I put on the smallest *Baetis* I had in my box, sat down on the bank, flattened myself in the wet meadow grass, slid feet-first into the lake like a corpse being tipped down a plank.

The ripple pushed the trout back a few yards, but didn't seem to particularly bother them; in their eyes, I was merely another elk or moose come to drink. I could see now there was a pattern to their swirling; they were moving in a counterclockwise circle between a dead log to my right, the drop-off straight ahead of me, and the inlet stream to my left.

Cutthroats have the endearing habit of being difficult to frighten, but they make up for this by being inordinately fussy; these fish could get a very clear, detailed look at the insects they were feeding on, and rejected every imitation I tried. I went through pattern after pattern, trying desperately to find a winner; it was no trick at all to get a fly in place well ahead of a cruiser, but they swam right beneath it without blinking.

In the meantime the family cheering section was if anything even more involved. Up high on the bank, they could see the fish even plainer than I could, and each time one swam toward my fly they were convinced it was coming up to it, and so screamed at me to strike.

Talk about pressure! I wanted to catch one for them, wanted this very badly, and yet the more I pressed, the more indifferent those trout became, to the point where I had to forcibly stop myself from lunging forward and grabbing one by the tail. Celeste—giving up on me, but tactful enough not to admit this—called that she was going around to the other side of the lake, where we had left our packs and lunches. "Good luck, Dad," she said—then she was gone.

The kids, having more faith, squatted down on their haunches to see what would happen. I'd been fishing a 4X tippet until then, but it was obvious now that in the placid water this was far too heavy, so I switched over to the longest 6X tippet I thought I could cast. The submerged log was the favorite place for the biggest fish to linger, though if I hooked one there I would have major problems. Still, it seemed my only option. I edged around toward the inlet so I wouldn't hook the backcast on the kids, then changed flies one last time. One of my *Baetis* was more beat-up looking than the others, crippled and squished the way trout like, and this is what I ended up tying on.

I false cast out the right amount of line, then let the fly drop beside the submerged log, staring toward it as intently as I've ever stared toward anything in my life.

"One's coming, Daddy!" Matthew shouted from the bank.

"Oh, my gosh!" Erin yelled. "It's going to—"

Take it! The moment I realized this the fly was gone, and the moment the fly was gone my arm came up and the fish was on. It was one of the biggest trout—there was no mistaking that deep, solid kind of take. My first reaction, even before I was con-scious of the kids shouting in delight behind me, was to get enough softness in my line to absorb what I knew would be that first hard double shake of his head, not be broken off right at the start.

I managed to do this, but it was hardly the end of my prob-lems. The log stuck out of the water like a tank trap deliberately planted to vex me, and a second after getting the necessary soft-ness in the line I was faced with the job of getting just the right amount of tightness in to turn the trout away from danger. Through some miracle I pulled this off, or perhaps it was the fish who did it to himself; faced with the choice of fleeing under the log or fleeing toward the drop-off, the fish picked the drop-off— and a moment later he was out in front of me with plenty of clear, empty water on each side.

So intent was I on keeping up with all this, so focused on the trout, it was only now that those excited shouts got through to my ears. The kids were war-dancing on the bank, jumping in ecstasy, their hands pressed down on their hats, yelling each time the trout turned. Across the lake, hidden from us by the trees, Celeste heard all the shouting, realized at once what must have happened, gathered the packs up and came running back as fast as she could.

The longer I had the trout on the more confident I felt about him, and yet this was dangerous, too, since to take him for granted on so fine a tippet would inevitably be to lose him. Then, too, I had left my net back in the car, so there was the problem of landing him. Leading him carefully back toward the log but in closer to me than last time, I waded around so I stood between him and deeper water, then slowly closed in on him as I took back line, until finally I had him resting within inches of the steep muddy bank.

"Bring him in, Daddy! Bring him in!"

Smart up to now, steady and patient, the sight of the huge fish so close to me made me lose my composure, and I all but threw myself at him, the bow wave of my lunge making him ride up onto the grass as prettily as if I had planned it that way in the first place.

"You've got him, Daddy! Got him!"

I was sweating at this stage, exhausted, with hardly the strength to climb out next to the fish. The kids came plunging down the cliff to stare, reach out their fingers to touch him on the side, see he was real. Celeste was there now, too, panting, sweating more than I was but yelling in happiness as she fumbled in the pack for our camera.

We photographed it, the kids squatting behind me as I held him up, then—each one holding out a hand to have a part in it, count coup with the trout's strength—released him gently down the bank and watched as he swam away. It was only then that the father in me took over from the fisherman—and I could relax enough to see what I should have seen all along: my kids dancing in victory on the bank, Celeste beaming proudly . . . and not just them, but the wildflowers in the meadow grass, the pines that started behind the lake, the mountains in the distance . . . the wide, unspoiled Yellowstone country, the warmth and majesty of which we only now fully appreciated thanks to its magic embodiment in that fish . . . how it all coalesced into a huge and comprehensible planet of brightness, me lying there on the grass with my eyes closed under the dizzying press of it, a triumphant Hercules who would gladly take ten such planets on his shoulders, my kids in my arms as we wrestled and hugged in sheer delight.

Put it down as the happiest, proudest moment in a man's fishing life? Sure, go ahead, but it was a lot more than that, too. The happiest moment in his *entire* life.

PART FIVE

The Long Autumn

Private Water

I HARDLY KNEW FISHING CLUBS EXISTED until I was invited to fish one. Occasionally I'd come across references in a fishing book to the old "club" water, hear of such along trout streams in the Catskills or on the Restigouche, clubs that took up many thousands of Maine acres or owned the rights to an improbably high number of Quebec lakes. I always associated them with high rollers, timber barons, old money, not my kind of world at all, and I was slow to pick up on the fact that fishing clubs exist on a much more humble and enjoyable scale as well, particularly in Vermont.

I'm thinking of the kind of fishing club that got its start back in the 1890s, when hill farms were being abandoned and entire mountain valleys could be bought up for a song. Shares would be issued in a corporation (doctors, lawyers, teachers, the local gentry, though a rural, likable enough one), an engineer hired, a rock and earthen dam erected across the valley's stream, a pond created, a clubhouse cobbled together, rules and regulations drawn up, an Indian name chosen to give just the right rustic flavor—and then the trout put in the pond, brookies usually, ones that were already dwelling in the stream, supplemented by larger fish taken from a nearby lake, transported by horse and wagon over rutted dirt roads in milk cans, the canoes and rowboats coming in on the next trip . . . a caretaker hired to watch over these and keep the wood box full, his wife taken on in summer to cook the meals . . . and there, Club Abenaki (Mohegan, Algonquian, Minnehaha) was in operation.

The trick was to *keep* it in operation, change it as little as possible through things like land booms, depressions, and world wars. The result is that there exists today in Vermont six or seven clubs that have changed so little since the 1890s you half expect Teddy Roosevelt to meet you at the door, or Calvin Coolidge at any rate, wearing his favorite fishing hat, and on his face the kind of thin, yet comfortable smile he let only his friends see in these precious moments at ease.

This is not just fantasy; the club I was invited to is proud of having had Silent Cal as one of its earliest members, and the very first thing I was shown when I arrived was the president's battered fishing hat hanging ready on its peg in the event his ghost should ever need it.

Catument I'll call this; on the smaller end of the fishing-club scale, it could still stand as representative of any. Its pond is about four acres in size, stocked with brookies and rainbows that grow just big enough to be interesting. The clubhouse was constructed partly of an old schoolhouse that was pulled by wagons up from town, and it sits on a rising lawn above the water, so old, so brown and weathered, it seems not only an organic part of the slope, but the fitting centerpiece of a compact and quiet valley where the land, sky, and water seem perpetually anchored in the early autumn of 1895.

That's outside. Inside, the identifying characteristic of any good fishing club is in the furnishings, the knickknacks, the pictures that hang lopsided on the walls. They have to be old and vaguely corny (a genuine antique would look out of place) and they have to be arranged with no thought whatsoever for effect. Catument gets top marks in this respect. Fishing cartoons from the thirties and forties hang on the walls, the H. T. Webster kind that play off the old fishing widow jokes or the small boy with worms. Mixed in with these are badly focused photos taken when color film was in its infancy, handwritten lists of bird sightings, a page or two from ancient fishing logs showing enormous one-day catches . . . and then a fireplace warm with a fire that hasn't gone out in a hundred years, the kitchen with its oversize zinc sink, the cupboard full of tumblers that have the smoky patina even clear glass takes on if you pour enough bourbon into it over the years . . . and then (glass in hand now, going back out to the club's main room) the piano that hasn't been tuned in fifty years, the boxes of snelled flies resting on top (Parmachene Belles, Edson Tigers, Montreals), the playing cards, the Scrabble games, the old magazines . . . the wobbly rocker, the wobbly card tables, the dilapidated couch . . . all of these giving the kind of feel it would be impossible to duplicate without at least seventy years of happy and relaxed usage, and a place I fell in love with the moment I walked in.

Terry Boone, my friend and host, is the club's historian, guiding spirit, and very much its chief attraction, at least for this visitor. Short and trim, bearded like a sea captain, the kind of stylish dresser once described as "dapper," he's a preacher's son from West Virginia who's entirely self-taught—the kind of man who can run a radio station with one hand while inventing a best-selling board game with the other, finding time along the way to consult on political campaigns, volunteer for a dozen charities, and take on the salmon-restoration effort of one of the largest conservation organizations in the country. Catument is the only place where you have a chance of catching him motionless, at least for a few minutes; after unpacking our groceries (Catument doesn't have a cook; members bring their own food and prepare it family style in the kitchen), he had a few projects to talk over with the caretaker, so I grabbed my fly rod and headed down to the pond alone.

When the fishing is on at the club's pond you can catch dozens, without regard to flies or tactics; when it's off, the fish are extraordinarily fussy, and it's easy to get skunked. No matter how long stocked trout live in a stream, they tend to remain at the same low level of imbecility, whereas in a pond they become very smart very fast, and these Catument rainbows, get a September midge hatch going, can be inscrutable opponents for even fly fishers of long experience.

This is rowboat fishing—add that to the soothing, relaxed effect the club induces. I rowed to the east end of the pond, got a good look at the osprey that camps out there in a dead pine, then let the breeze drift me back toward the dam, picking up some nice fish on a Hare's Ear nymph twitched just below the surface.

Terry had the swordfish on the grill when I got back, but there was still time to help myself to some cheese and crackers, sip some bourbon on the porch with his other guests, who had only just arrived. One of the things you learn about fishing clubs is that though the ostensible reason for their existence is fishing, *talking* is of even more importance—the kind of relaxed medium-small talk that can only be done in a setting of rocking chairs, wood fires, and porches. The subject is often fishing, sure, but it's never limited to this, and usually has a way of coming around to subjects freely suggested by what can be seen off the porch: osprey and deer, sunsets and foliage, the natural small talk a Vermont valley tends to provide in autumn without any prompting.

This was my first experience of Catument. The second was when Terry got married there—a bright October afternoon of such perfection that tears came to your eyes well before the actual ceremony, to see how rich and sweet the autumnal note could be played. Chairs had been set up on the lawn leading down to the pond, with an end table taken from the porch for a makeshift altar. Karen Kayen, Terry's bride, is a good friend of ours, a woman we admire hugely, so it was a perfect match in this respect as well, and just to see Terry's happy smile as she joined him by the pond was enough to get tears going in those who had successfully resisted the foliage.

Karen's father stood to the side playing a soft, lyric sonata on his violin; as the notes faded away across the pond, the minister stepped in and had them recite their vows. Many of those in attendance were dedicated fly fishers, and they all—how shall I put this?—stared with special *intentness* at the pond with its trout, so a good half of the congregation seemed to be leaning toward the water, as if caught in the breeze. None of them leaned far enough that they actually *went* fishing, but I know what they were thinking since I was thinking it myself. Anticipating this, in a very clever piece of strategy, Terry and Karen had arranged for *gravlax* to be served with champagne immediately after the ceremony was over—those rich salmon appetizers there is simply no resisting. It was the best wedding I've ever attended, hands down. The pond, the foliage, the warm October breeze; given a choice, who wouldn't wish to be wafted toward their future from a setting so fine?

If Catument is one of the smallest and simplest trout clubs in Vermont, then Lake Tanso is among the largest and plushest. With three ponds and a connecting brook trout stream, several hundred acres in one of the steepest, most remote notches in the Green Mountains, a hundred-year-old clubhouse that can accommodate seventy overnight guests, and a loyal membership devoted to keeping things the way they've always been, Tanso is one of those miraculous Shangri-Las you have no suspicion of until you're actually standing in its center, then, upon leaving, have trouble believing you were ever actually in at all.

I came to it first on a rainy September morning when the clouds hung so low over the ridges they seemed to merge into the placid water on the pond's far end. There was a fire going in the fireplace (three times bigger than Catument's, with three times as many rockers pulled up in front), but the lodge was deserted, and I had to poke around the empty rooms until I found my host, Dick Connors, sitting where I should have figured he'd be sitting—out on the porch with the geraniums, rocking contentedly with his pipe, staring out at the rings pushed into the water by rising trout.

"Good to see you!" he said, getting up to shake my hand. Then, a second later, reaching behind him to the wooden pegs that held his rod: "What are we waiting for? Let's catch some fish!"

The largest pond is over eight acres, and thick with brook trout and rainbows. They reproduce naturally here, at least the brookies, and each season fish are taken upward of three and four pounds. As at most fishing clubs, there's a continual debate in progress about whether the pond's natural food supply should be supplemented by feeding, and at Tanso those in the proactive camp win. Two coop-like contraptions are mounted on platforms on either end of the pond. Inside is fish food, and an automatic timing device that twice a day casts pellets out in a broad circle. The trout have learned to expect this, and the shark-like frenzy that erupts when the timer goes off is something to see. Visiting fishermen immediately try to catch one of these monsters, but

it's impossible, even if you have a fly that resembles a food pel-
let; like junk-food addicts, these fish can spot the difference
between a real Twinkie and a fake one in a quick supercilious
glance, and the only thing to do is wait until their jag wears off,
and a size 24 Gray Midge once again begins to look palatable.

Dick is a school superintendent in a midsize city that's seen
better days—no more grueling a job now exists in this country.
At Tanso, out in the boat, he seems like a man who has had a
very heavy weight temporarily lifted from his shoulders; when it
comes to the ponds, the fish, the mountains, he wears his heart
on his sleeve.

"Deep spot here, might try a leech. Tommy North caught a
four-pound rainbow here last week. Not a bad summer—decent
hatches until August. Hey, is that a bear? Saw one yesterday
when I got up to row coffee out to some of the old fellas.
Whoops, rise up ahead, two o'clock. Think you can reach him if
I turn us around? God, I love the look of those clouds! Smell
those leaves!"

Only on Scottish lochs, fishing under a similar kind of
mist, have I sensed such perfect self-containment, as if trout
were the only purpose in life, water the medium in which the
purpose dwells, a rowboat the magically suspended derrick by
which the purpose can be mined. And, as mentioned, I love
fishing in rowboats. Tanso has a whole fleet of them, docked
inside a long weathered boathouse that dates from the turn of
the century. Lapstreaked, the long wooden kind with two pairs
of davits, they're just heavy enough to withstand some wind
(any good rowboat is heavy), and just broad enough you can
stand up in them to cast. There is something about the yielding sensation a rowboat creates in the water, the way it
responds so fast to the slightest leverage, that makes you feel
as if you're combing the water, and it's the kind of intimate ges-

ture that makes you feel perfectly at one with it, a craft the water somehow *likes*.

The various streamers of mist eventually found one another, fell as a solid curtain of rain that drove us back to the boathouse. From the club's long porch came a deep drawn-out sound I thought at first was the call of a moose (or the mountains yawning), but which turned out to be one of the young women who worked in the kitchen blowing on a conch shell to signal it was time for lunch. And what a lunch. Homemade potpie, a huge spinach salad, Ben & Jerry's Cherry Garcia washed down by coffee laced with good Vermont cream. Tanso is the kind of club where wonderfully prepared meals are a big part of the attraction—not just the food, but the easy kind of talk that comes when the fishing is right outside the window and you know it will wait until you're done.

A few other members drifted in now, including Dick's mother and father, who live not far away. The club has members all over the country, but the ones who live within driving distance use it the most, especially in autumn. Dick's father showed me around the clubhouse. Like Catument's, it's decorated with old black-and-white photos from the club's early days, cartoons cut out of newspapers fifty years old, joke flies made of coat hangers, duck feathers, and ribbons, piles of old word games and Reader's Digest condensed books. The bedrooms are small and simply furnished—the bedsteads the old-fashioned iron kind even a hurricane couldn't shake, and on top are folded army blankets of thick green wool.

We fished again after lunch. Three or four boats were out now, but they hardly dented our sense of solitude. That's another nice thing about rowboats: so slow is their locomotion that there is a natural tendency to remain pretty much in the same spot, focus only on the water within reach . . . and Dick and I talked about whether this might be the simple low-tech solution to overcrowding on trout water everywhere—require everyone to fish in rowboats.

Still-water fishing is static enough that it bores some people, and often in springtime it bores me, but not in autumn; there's a relaxed feel that goes down well with the weather, the whole autumnal package of pleasurably sad regrets. Back in the shallows where the inlet came in I lost a nice fish, then landed one that was big enough to make up for my disappointment—a brookie dressed for autumn, with so much color and vibrancy I was half afraid to take it in my hand, convinced that, like the bright golden leaves that clung to the trees above us, its beauty would burn. All the more reason to release it in the water; I reached my fingers down to the hook, twisted it gently, and saw the scarlet drop back into the amber-colored transparency from which it had emerged.

Every now and then I'll be asked, in what I'm sure is a deliberately offhand manner, whether or not I might be interested in applying for membership at one of these clubs. It's tempting, since the financial end of it is surprisingly reasonable. At Catument, you pay for an initial share plus yearly dues; at Tanso, you also pay each time you come, at least for room and board; in this respect, it functions like a small private hotel, so there's an economic incentive to have as members young families who will use the lodge often.

So far I've always turned down these invites with thanks. We have many of these kinds of delights very close to home free of charge, and the prospect of being on a waiting list for five years or more, *any* waiting list, is more than my patience can handle. I'm not a particularly clubbable sort of guy, which is also part of it, though perhaps I'm being overly shy in this respect; sitting on those porches, sharing that bourbon, I've found the members of both clubs to be an interesting and surprisingly varied sort, and if the conversation turns momentarily to the events of the larger world, you're apt to find you're talking to as many liberal Democrats as reactionary Republicans, the one common denominator being a healthy conservatism toward any changes in the club's own domain.

There are lessons in this kind of stewardship that are applicable to public waters. The state of Vermont owns a pond over in the east-central part of the state, the site of a fishing club that couldn't pay its taxes. It's now run as a fly-fishing-only park (pay as you go, reservations required, two-fish limit), and an excellent one, combining the access of public fishing with the restricted numbers of a club. I fish there often in the fall, again using rowboats (aluminum ones, alas, a material that should be used only to wrap sandwiches), and find it has very much the same feel as Tanso, even to the clubhouse, which is not only used for conservation-related conferences and wildlife seminars, but offers simple lodgings for the night.

The great days of a state's acquiring park land through tax sales and eminent domain are over, I suppose, but it's an idea that would certainly be a good one for these overcrowded days— a state taking a few ponds or streams that are already in its possession and operating them on this controlled-access basis. I would never want to see all the fishing operated this way—our tradition of public access is too valuable and ingrained, and gives every fly fisher a stake in protecting all our water—but some such arrangement in each trout-fishing state would offer quality fishing and a club kind of feel, this time to a much wider cross-section of fly fishers. A place that is deliberately anachronistic, removed from the competitive pressure that mars so much of our current fishing? Well yes—why not? If I haven't said so already, pond fishing in a rowboat for wild and catchable trout is the best way ever invented for interesting a young person in fishing, and to do this in a setting where fly fishing is honored as the simple, traditional pastime it should be makes the experience all the more vital.

Some people in Vermont find even private club waters far too public, and do most of their fishing right at home. A bulldozer is hired with a crusty old-timer who's been at this game for years, an acre-sized hole dug out where the clay lies thickest, a stream damned if there is one or an overflow pipe hooked up to a reliable artesian well, ten-inch trout ordered from one of the fish farms or feed stores, a willow or two planted on the banks, a little dock knocked together out of lumber—and there, you're in business, with your own private trout water you can stroll down to any time you want.

I'm surprised at how many of these lie scattered about these hills; driving, I'll glance through the trees and catch a quick glimpse of a compact bowl of silvery water tucked away into the landscape where it's all but invisible. Many of these contain large trout, rainbows of seven or eight pounds (my guess is the best fly fishing in New England is in private ponds), but sometimes the environment remains a little artificial and forced, so it's like you're fishing for pets in an aquarium, not catching them so much as dipping them out.

The best private ponds are the most natural—those where the water is gently borrowed from a stream and gently returned. I have a friend (let's call him, uh, Tom) who lives in a narrow valley well up in the hills. Above his property is the source of a small stream: a beaver flowage that is always marshy, even in seasons of drought. Where the flowage begins to narrow into a definite channel his property begins, and a hundred yards below this, many years ago now, a previous owner built an earthen dam housing an outflow pipe and a wooden spillway. The resulting pond isn't much over an acre, and fits into the flowage perfectly, being little more than a natural widening, the slightest pause, in the water's rush down to the valley floor three miles away.

Native brook trout live in the beaver flowage, and in times of high water will come down into the pond and do just fine; there are also brookies in the pool just below the dam, attracted by the cold and reliable spillage. Tom stocks the pond once a year with several dozen brook trout and five or six rainbows, and these grow to serious size, without his having to feed them. I've caught twenty-inch brook trout here, a twenty-four-inch rainbow, and they have the kind of thickness and strength you see on fish out in Montana.

If the pond fits perfectly into the natural order here, it also fits perfectly into the man-made one, which is what gives a private pond much of its charm. The lawn slopes down to the water from the house; a birdhouse-festooned willow overhangs the bank on which a rowboat is pulled up, waiting for guests to help themselves; the kids have left their butterfly nets about, and out in the middle of the pond floats a Wiffle ball driven there in last night's game. Tom constructed a dock near the spillway that lets you cover the deepest part of the pond with an easy cast; playing a fish here, if you give even a little yell, everyone will rush down from the house to see whether it's big enough to get excited about and stick around until it's landed.

Charming, of course—what fly fisher hasn't dreamed of having this kind of action so close at hand? And yet it's not without its worries. Careless road work will silt up the flowage, turn the pond muddy for days. Poachers will fish it when the family is gone, keep everything they catch. The dam is a constant source of worry—every now and then you read in the papers about one going out, causing a destructive flood (the great Johnstown flood, remember, was caused by the rupture of a dam at a private fishing club). Natural as the pond is, it suffers from a natural kind of predation—heron and otter can wipe out the fish in a very short time. Over the years a pond can become so precious it's hard to leave when it comes time to move on. I have friends who, faced with pressures to move to better jobs or better schools, found their pond had become so integral a part of their happiness they could not bear leaving it behind, and so took cuts in pay or accepted the fact that they would have to spend long parts of their day chauffeuring their kids to and from a distant school. Love any small portion of the landscape and an obligation falls on you to take it seriously, cherish it, protect it, and in this day and age the burden can seem exhausting.

Is it worth it? I know Tom would say yes, even though he fishes the pond only occasionally now, taking most of his pleasure from seeing his friends and his kids catch the trout he all but knows by name. He's given me a standing invite to fish it anytime I want, which usually turns out to be three or four times a year. In April, just after the ice melts, I enjoy going out with him in his canoe, to catch fish at a time when there's nowhere else to catch fish, become reacquainted with that firm tugging pressure in the arm, that dancing rod tip, the wet spring, and coil of color in my hand. In June, waiting for a windless, cloudy day, I enjoy taking fish after fish right on top with my little two-weight. A bit later in the summer I'll bring my father over, help him catch some trout his poor eyesight wouldn't allow him to catch anywhere else.

My favorite time to fish the pond is in October after a season spent chasing difficult and fussy fish. Tom will be at work, his family will be off at school, and it will just be me, the row-boat, and the trout—generous and eager fish who don't require much persuading to come leaping over to my side. Behind me the bank with the pines will be golden beneath fallen needles; by the dam the sumac and willows will have turned red and the brightest yellow; up in the shallows the brookies, the anxious ones, will be already spawning, turning in tight circles of the utmost concentration and intensity—a concentration not even a rowboat, not even the streamer that takes trout so easily just a few yards away, will manage to shake. These are gorgeous fish, the males coral and fiery, with hooked jaws that let you know what you're dealing with is passion, serious passion, that will stand no interference from the puny likes of you.

Part of my pleasure in fishing here is a selfish one, to have a trout-filled body of water all to myself, and yet it's not the snob-bery, I-have-it-and-you-don't kind of selfishness, but something that carries with it gratitude and thanks. Thanks for what? For being able to concentrate so directly on the fish, know there will be no interruption in the intense and important business of try-ing to understand the workings of this small cup of wildness, coax it occasionally to my purpose. You realize, in the end, that even this homey body of water carries with it as much mystery as a large and untamed lake, the mystery all life seems to contain at its healthiest, something you sense very strongly, feel you can all but pull from the water with a quick dipping hand, and yet even on a perfect autumn day like this one, borne and uplifted on the backs of willing trout, will never quite be able to grasp.

All trout water is private water, seen in this light. A trout tugs us and from habit we tug back—and yet how much better to let the fish, the dweller in the mystery, pull us down into its center so we can see for ourselves what it's like to live in paradise, even the paradise that comes to us one precious acre at a time.

September 18

PERFECT CONDITIONS. The sailor asks that the wind blow from just the right quarter, at just the right speed; the kayaker that the river level be propitious, neither too high nor too low; the mountaineer that the weather fronts behave themselves; the photographer, that the light be soft; the hunter, that the biological rhythm that animates the game he seeks has them fully on the move . . . and yet the fly fisher is fussier than any of these, because when he wishes for a perfect day he speaks of all these things combined, wind, water, weather, light, and instinct, so a perfect day for fishing is perhaps the rarest, most precious circumstance in any of the outdoor sports.

How rare? There's a day I look forward to all year long, yet only get perhaps one season out of five, so fussy are its requirements. It needs to be a day in the second or third week of September, when the Connecticut that runs past my home has been scoured by a long summer's flowage, so it shines brighter than it does at any other time of year, with a good three or four feet more of transparent depth. You need a frost in the early part of the week—the water must have noticeably, but not drastically cooled. It can't be past the equinox, since the storms we get then muddy things up. The wind must be from the south—from the north, you may as well stay at home. Most important of all, it must be a day when it's significantly warmer than it has been, so it feels like midsummer has been returned to you on a golden platter, with apologies for that trick of frost.

Get all these things without exception and it means the best smallmouth fishing of the year, a day when their biological clock is so exuberantly on it's as if you're fishing a solid river of bassiness, the water having by this perfect stirring of variables taken on striped bars and golden flesh and chevroned fins and glistening scales and extravagant muscle. It's something I anticipate all summer long, deliberately avoiding all engagements or appointments so I can be here at the right moment . . . and then spend September keeping track of all the various factors, trying not to get my hopes up but getting them up anyway, feeling good when that first early frost comes, feeling even better when it's followed by warmer weather, rooting for the wind to stay in the south, all but applying body English to the atmosphere, trying to bend and shape the elements to my purpose, if only for a single day.

When I woke up yesterday morning I thought I had the combination I was looking for. We'd had our frost earlier in the week, the northwest wind had swung around to the south, and there was a nostalgic stillness in the air that harkened back toward August. A heavy fog was fine with me, since one of the other ingredients in this kind of perfection is the slow warming of the shallows where the bass roam, and you get this when there's enough moisture in the air to act as a gentle scrim. By eleven, conditions would be just right, giving me time to work on my novel and thereby achieve that other cornerstone of perfection: going out to the river with a conscience that's clear.

I suppose there was some self-congratulation in my attitude—that I was clever enough not only to recognize perfection when it came, but to keep my calendar open for its arrival—and thus enough pride that it was goeth-ing for a falleth-ing. I had the canoe up on the car, had my rod stowed, my poppers packed, a lunch ready . . . I was heading back to the house for my hat, feeling the kind of happy urgency that transforms a middle-aged man into a ten-year-old kid . . . when there was a hard, sudden tap on my shoulder, the kind that fate often likes to deliver aurally, in this case as the frantic yipping of an aging retriever who had chosen that moment to impale herself on a rusty strand of barbed wire out on the far end of our stone wall.

At thirteen, Cider is as lively as a puppy and a bit nearsighted—a bad combination when it comes to stumbling into barbed wire. She'd cut herself badly on the back of the leg, and it was obvious it was going to take stitches to close the wound. This was the kind of thing I hadn't figured into my calculations, and made me realize that my criteria for perfection, though stringent enough, were nowhere near adequate, since they hadn't taken into consideration the chances of life becoming snared in the various entanglements that seem spontaneously improvised just to ruin your day.

Our vet lives twenty miles north. Cider did fine once I got her on the back seat; her expression was a combination of guilt and embarrassment, in the usual way of goldens, and every now and then to comfort her I had to twist my head around and say something reassuring. I was vexed, of course—more than vexed. Impatient, pissed, furious. The further I drove—the greater the distance I was putting between me and the day I had planned— the angrier I became, to the point where in order not to go flying off the road altogether I had to get a moral hold on myself, start figuring out what was going on.

Part of this was easy—the normal vexation anyone feels when their plans go awry. This was multiplied (let's say doubled) by the fact that it came at a particularly bad, or rather *good* time: the perfect day I'd been waiting for all season. This is something any fly fisher will understand, something so intrinsically part of the game it's hardly worth mentioning, but after this things became a bit murkier, more personal, and it was a while before I figured them out.

My reasoning went something like this . . .

Normally I'm the luckiest of fishermen, someone who can go fishing almost any time he wants. To suddenly have this taken away from me—to discover my charmed fishing life was mortal after all, and could be lost not to a major catastrophe, but a minor one—was a hard thing to swallow, though not without its value as a kind of therapeutic lesson, a reminder of just how remarkably lucky I am most of the time. Okay, I could understand this, reason was doing its job. But not being able to go fishing, even in this one slight instance, was making me overreact in a way that went far beyond this, and I finally realized it was because it made me remember a time when I couldn't go fishing at all—the long years I was stuck in the suburbs, someone who only dreamed of fishing, but for reasons too complicated and difficult to go into here, hardly ever went out. This only changed in my thirties when I broke away from that life, moved north to the country and was, quite literally, reborn.

Thinking in these terms, it's easy to see what was at stake: even a small threat to the kind of life I'd established inflamed the old scar tissue, burned as something I had to smother immediately with all the emotion I was capable of mustering—not a small vexation in an otherwise fine day, but a threat to my very existence.

And further. Fishing, right from the start, was an expression of the rebellious half of my nature, the anti-establishment part of me, the kid who went fishing when the rest of his generation stormed ROTC buildings or did drugs—the passion in me that is partly a finger jabbed toward the conforming philistine materialistic culture I've so thoroughly despised, actively when younger, latently today. Give my new life even one small check and the old emotion comes flooding back, the fury that used to possess me in my twenties when I realized the life I imagined was passing me by.

Poor Cider! There she was bearing stoically something that must have caused considerable pain, and there her master was gripping the steering wheel like he wanted to throttle anything and everything he could get his hands around, never mind the aching dog. But I got her to the vet without ramming into anyone. I held her as Dr. Wheeler examined her, helped where I could when he sewed her up, carried her back out and laid her gently on the back seat—and like a pet-ambulance driver, raced her back home in record time.

One o'clock—only two hours lost. I got Cider settled in the mud room, drove down River Road to the dirt launching area owned by the Nature Conservancy, loaded up the canoe with my fly rod and poppers, shoved myself off into the river. The sun had it shining in that penny brightness I had reckoned on; below the canoe, as I pried it out toward the wooded island that's my favorite spot, I could see small bass swimming over the sandy bottom, with the kind of heads-up alertness, eagerness, and hunger you see in June during spawning and then not again until a fall day like this one.

The river here is only slightly wider than where I fish for trout, and yet there's enough breadth now that it seems a much weightier proposition, something that doesn't rush and dance but sweeps and proceeds. With the breeze from the south, the surface had those little crisp folds that come at such short intervals they make the canoe seem like it's on a moving ramp, and in no time at all I was drifting past the weedbed at the island's upper edge, attached to a smallmouth that had taken the Olive Zonker I'd been trolling out the stern.

I caught six bass on the first seven casts—*that's* what I mean by perfection—and with every one I felt myself relax even more. Perfection? Though from long experience I recognize the conditions that prompt this, I'm still confused as to what exactly is going on, at least as far as the bass are concerned. Yes, the water has cooled off, and their metabolism must welcome this. Yes, the water is clearer, and those crayfish become an easier target for them in the shallows. But how do they know the wind is from the south and why does this please them? How do they sense the relatively low barometric pressure, since by rising or falling a few inches in the river they can make it anything they want? How do they sense winter is coming, by what mechanism or instinct? More specifically, how come they sense winter so strongly on the most summer-like days? It's reasonable to expect a feeding binge from a creature who is faced with seven months when it hardly eats at all, but why is the frenzy so closely tied to such fussy factors? Fishing magazines have always made a great deal over this feeding binge, so it's become an article of faith to most fishermen, but myself, I've rarely seen it, find fish in autumn to be at their moodiest, with this one specific exception: on the right day in September the smallmouth on the Connecticut River go absolutely wild.

As I came around the tip of the island my lee disappeared and the breeze pushed the canoe over toward the Vermont shore. This was fine with me—the bass line up there along boulders dumped down the bank when the railroad was built well over a hundred and fifty years ago. There are old telegraph wires, too, strung on sunken poles that dip right into the river, making it

seem as if this whole vanished infrastructure, trains and telegraph both, have as their only function a soggy communication
with sunken ghosts.

As I drifted, I cast—in autumn you can sometimes pick up
a sunbathing bass right in the middle of the river—and cast
standing up. This is against all the canoeing rules, of course, but
I've been using this Old Town for so many years it's become an
easy and comfortable position, and there's something daring and
stately about it I enjoy, like riding a surfboard towed by dolphins.

Along the bank the wild honeysuckle had turned brown; a
bittern, staying just ahead of me, blended perfectly with the
color, and it took the crisp rattle of leaves for me to pick him up
again twenty yards downstream. Where the bank steepened into
a sandy cliff I pulled the canoe in and waded the last ten feet to
shore. It's a good place to relax, since the bank slopes back like
a chaise lounge; as I drank my tea, ate my sandwich, my neck
was tickled by sand rolling down from the holes left by nesting
swallows at the top of the bank.

I was in no hurry to go back out—if anything, the perfect day
was turning out to be a little too warm, and so not quite perfect
after all. A temperature of seventy-three makes the bass remember winter is coming and gets them feeding; a temperature of
seventy-six makes them think it's August again and turns them
perversely sluggish. I knew it was almost certainly the last day of
bass fishing for the season. The forecast called for it to turn
sharply colder, and already I could see coral-tinged thunder-
heads moving across the mountains to the north.

I caught more fish after lunch, though they didn't come
quite so fast. On days like this one the smallmouth want a bul-
let-nosed popper, the slider kind with rubber legs, and they want
it fished without any motion other than what the current does to
those dangling legs. Casting these can be tricky. You need a mix

of force and finesse to do it properly; force in ramming it sidearm under the overhanging white pine that line the shore; finesse (applied at just the last moment) in making sure the popper enters the thin window you're aiming for, the nine or ten inches between the top of the water and the bottom of the trees.

It's funny about trout and bass. As much as I love the former, I never experience anything even remotely close to a fellow feeling for them, and most of my interest revolves around finding them and getting them to strike. With smallmouth it's different. I have a very strong fellow feeling for them, and it comes primarily during the fight. Have I ever written about the glories of a smallmouth's fight? No fish, neither largemouth nor rainbow nor striper nor salmon, punches as hard as a full-bodied smallmouth. The explosive strike followed by those wild unpredictable first seconds when the fish sometimes jumps (maybe a tailwalk, maybe the classic cartwheel, maybe a wild vault back toward the bank) and sometimes dives, then the frantic second pull, followed immediately by the first seriously deep plunge, getting into your backing it dives so deep, coming back up again entirely on its own and jumping again at a distance, then plunging again *if* it's still on, plunging a third time, still reserving enough strength to jump one last time close to the canoe, and even at the very end, just when you reach down for him, retaining enough pugnacity it can flail at your hand and get away.

What is the fellow feeling in all this, the connection that makes me know exactly what the bass is experiencing? I wouldn't have known what to link it to, not until that little episode with Cider, that frantic overreaction on my part when it became likely I wouldn't be able to go fishing. Why look further? The bass fights with frantic and uncompromising purpose, and I share a portion of that frantic quality myself, at least when it comes to the passion with which I approach my time out on the water. Yes,

I want a gentle, relaxed sport, one that involves myself, the river, the fish in a sometimes complicated, sometimes simple symbiosis, but how fiercely I want this, want this still. Bass and fisherman tug on opposite ends of the line, and yet on a ninety-nine and nine-tenths perfect September afternoon like this one, they end up striving toward the same kind of rebellious freedom, racing to see who gets there first.

Her Woods Still

ON A LATE SUMMER DAY in 1935, a schoolteacher from Massachusetts named Louise Dickinson neared the end of a vacation canoe trip through the Rangeley chain of lakes in western Maine. Her party was faced with a grueling portage—the five-mile length of the Rapid River, which connects Lower Richardson with Umbagog Lake at the bottom of the chain. The Rapid is said to be the most rapid river east of the Rockies, and an old dirt carry road parallels its unnavigable length; over the carry a man named Ralph Rich was picking up some extra money by ferrying canoe parties from one lake to the other with a 1924 Marmon touring car and makeshift trailer he had brought into the woods over the winter ice.

Louise and Ralph struck up a conversation, found immediately they had much in common. Ralph had sold some patent rights back in Chicago and had saved enough that he intended to spend the rest of his life in the woods; Louise's was an adventurous, nonconforming soul that until that moment had found little outlet. A few months later they were married and living along the Rapid River in an old summer house, miles from the nearest town, surrounded by thousands of acres of paper-company wilderness—a place Louise was to live for the next fifteen years, with long intervals (the longest, four years) when she never left the woods at all for "outside."

"During most of my adolescence," she begins her book, "specifically, between the time when I gave up wanting to be a brakeman on a freight train and the time when I decided to become an English teacher, I said, when asked what I was going to do with my life, that I was going to live alone in a cabin in the Maine woods and write."

Write is what she did, three books on her experiences along the Rapid River, beginning with the volume that sits beside me on the desk as I type: *We Took to the Woods*. Mine is the paperback edition of 1948, and the publishing history inside the front cover attests to the book's enormous popularity. First hardback edition from Lippincott in 1942, followed quickly by four more printings; an Atlantic Monthly condensed version published later that summer, and a Reader's Digest condensation in the fall; a Book-of-the-Month Club edition printed November 1942, with seven printings through 1944; a Liberty condensed version in 1943 and an Esquire condensed version in 1946; a Grosset and Dunlap hardback with four printings between 1946 and 1947; an Armed Services Edition in 1946; the Pocket Books paperback published in June 1948 . . . all of these, with their simple black-and-white photos (logging camp cooks, pulp-filled ponds, huge snowdrifts, craggy-looking Maine guides), their endpaper maps of the Rangeley region, the vaguely balsam, vaguely mildewed scent time has given them, being to this day the reliable staple of flea markets, library sales, and secondhand bookstores all throughout New England.

It's not hard to understand why her books were so popular. She's a good writer, with a good story to tell, Thoreau with a happy face, someone who was alive to the romance inherent in her situation, and yet managed to keep her prose and philosophy down-to-earth.

> I like to think of the lakes coming down from the north of us like a gigantic staircase to the sea. Kennebago to Range-ley to Cupsuptic, down they drop, level to level, through short, snarling rivers; Mooselukmeguntic to the Richard-sons to Pond-in-the-River, and through Rapid River to Umbagog, whence they empty into the Androscoggin and begin the long south-easterly curve back to the ocean. I like to say their names, and I wish I could make you see them—long, lonely stretches of water shut in by dark hills. There are a few narrow trails, but travel through the woods is so difficult, with the swamps and blowdowns and underbrush, that the lakes have remained what they were to the Indians, the main thoroughfares.

She was lucky enough to live there when the rough exuber-ance of the old logging days hadn't yet been killed off by modern industrial logging, and many of her best stories revolve around the shabby, put-upon loggers who, once they were in the woods, assumed almost mythological stature. She was also lucky in her family and friends: Ralph, her cantankerous, brilliantly improvi-sational husband; Gerrish, the family's hired man who became much more than that; Al and Larry Parsons, who acted as win-ter caretakers at Coburns, the fishing camp at the far end of the Carry Road; her son Rufus, a babe, quite literally, in the woods. She had a novelist's touch with them all. Judging by the photos of Louise herself, she was a plain but strong woman, with an open and approachable face, the kind of person who would be good in an emergency, with just enough tartness to keep you from underestimating her—and this is the quality that comes across in her books, so, reading them, you quickly become her friend.

These things help explain her popularity, but don't quite account for it all. You only have to look at the dates on the various editions, remember what was going on in the world then, to understand what underlay their extraordinary appeal. Louise Dickinson Rich lived in the woods all through the last years of the Depression and World War Two, concentrating on blueberry picking and salmon fishing and sap gathering when the rest of the world was involved with something very different. It's no wonder people found solace reading her books; to someone caught up in the dislocation and chaos of war, the story of a simple, uncomplicated life miles from anywhere must have seemed an irresistible daydream. She was aware of this herself, was quick to defend her books as something more than escapist fare ("We haven't tried to escape from anything. We have only exchanged one set of problems for another"), but it's clear that for hundreds of thousands of readers it was the chance to escape to the woods for a few hours via her books that made them so compelling.

Her philosophy, too. It's simple and simply stated, yet comes across with the kind of total sincerity that seems so rare and so precious during complex times. "I am free," she says, in concluding her first book. "All ordinary people like us, everywhere, are trying to find the same things. It makes no difference whether they are New Englanders or Texans or Malaysians or Finns. They all want to be left alone to conduct their own private search for a personal peace, a reasonable security, a little love, a chance to attain happiness through achievement. It isn't much to want, but I never came anywhere near to getting most of these things until we took to the woods."

I must have been thirteen or fourteen when I first came upon her books on the dusty lower shelves of our suburban library. In a time of general prosperity her books had lost some of their popularity, and one of the first things I noticed was that none of the books had been taken out in six or seven years. I fell in love with them, of course, and how could it be otherwise, since already by that time living in the woods and writing was exactly what I wanted to do with my own life. Her books are of a type there is no shorthand name for, but which was once a flourishing genre. Henry Rowlands's account of living alone in the far north of Ontario, *Cache Lake Country*. Charlie Childs's still-readable account of building a summer home from scratch on the Maine Coast, *Roots in the Rock; The House on Nauset Marsh* by Wyman Richardson, and a dozen others, all of which seemed to be illustrated by Henry Bugbee Kane. These are not great books by any means, but they were all good books, and, like the tales Don Quixote read of chivalry, they played havoc with the fantasy of a boy who already loved woods, water, and hills, and yet was stuck in the concrete suburbs feeling the utter impotence, when it came to dreams, of being thirteen.

I was already a passionate fisherman; one of the things I discovered, reading Rich's books, was that the fishing camp she called Coburns (where she worked one spring to distract herself after Ralph's sudden tragic death) was now called Lakewood Camps. I sent away for their brochure—and for many years, right through my teens and twenties, I would get a postcard every May, with a picture of a pool on the Rapid River and big letters announcing THE ICE IS OUT AT MIDDLE DAM!

A teenager, I had no way of getting there, no one to take me, and even in my twenties I never had the chance to go, so that postcard, arriving every spring just when my hopes were at their strongest, took on a mocking quality, that grown to manhood I still should be so far from achieving even one of the smaller of my boyhood dreams: to fish the country Rich described.

And then I did move north, found myself living only a morning's drive from her part of western Maine. Now my excuse for not going was different . . . I told myself it's best to leave at least some childhood landscapes virgin and intact . . . but after a while this seemed overly refined, even silly, and when my friend Tom Ciardelli started telling me about the Rapid and its fly fishing for landlocks, I decided it was time to go, combine some fishing with some pilgrimage. One of the greatest pleasures in life is visiting a place you've fallen in love with through books, through imagination. Okay, the Rapid River isn't London or Venice or even the Allagash, but for a good many years it had teased and intrigued my wondering, and it was high time I saw it in person.

We went in late September, a week before the salmon season ended. Back along the Connecticut the leaves were just starting to turn, but once past Errol, once we crossed the Maine border and drove up the first step in the high inland plateau that dominates the state, the gold was everywhere, a wide rolling carpet spreading down toward the scraggly blue of Umbagog in the near distance to our left.

Lakewood Camps can be reached only by water; the drill is, reaching the small town of Andover, you go to the general store and call ahead so the boat can meet you at South Arm, the long southward finger of Lower Richardson Lake. There were a couple of cars parked on the gravel apron above the dock when we arrived; one of these was a state police car, the other a fish and game truck, but except for Tom making a joke about a game bust in progress we hardly gave these any thought.

Anyone who's read much Louise Dickinson Rich knows how important South Arm was to her entire way of life—virtually every trip outside went that way; most supplies, most visitors, came to the woods across the lake. On the bluff are some old weather-beaten garages that could certainly date from 1940, where those living in the woods kept their outside cars. On a late September day like this one, with no one around, a good chop cutting up the blue, Lower Richardson seemed high, wild, and lonely, little changed from how it must have looked fifty years before.

We had carried our duffle bags and rod cases down to the dock, were standing there wondering if we had missed connections, when a small cabin cruiser entered the channel, slowed, then edged sideways toward the dock.

We could see three men aboard—a man behind the wheel, a state trooper, a game warden—and it was a few more seconds before we noticed there was a fourth as well.

In the stern of the boat, riding so low we didn't at first see it, rested a tarpaulin-covered stretcher with a small pair of old-fashioned brown shoes sticking out one end. Tom and I both reached over to pull the boat in, and now, seeing this we involuntarily let go. "Give us room now," the trooper said quietly, and then without any other words being spoken, he took one end of the stretcher as the game warden took the other, and between them they carried the body up the steep ramp toward shore.

It was the Lakewood Camps boat all right; Stan Milton, the owner, helped us load our luggage, then briefly explained what had happened.

A ninety-two-year-old man had died, a longtime summer resident at one of the camps along shore. He'd come up for the salmon fishing and collapsed suddenly that morning getting into his boat. I did a quick calculation, realized he was a contemporary of Rich's, could very possibly have known her. Certainly, it was her kind of story—a bittersweet one, a fate that was tied closely to the land. As Stan steered the boat out into the open part of the lake, the engine became too noisy for us to talk about it any further, but we had agreed it wasn't a bad way to go, not at that age, not doing what he loved. His death, meeting us like that, gave a solemn quality to the landscape and seemed to place it even more solidly in times past.

Lakewood Camps sits on the edge of the lake a couple of hundred yards from Middle Dam, the old gated dam where the Rapid River spills down toward Pond-in-the-River. A weathered brown lodge with a wide verandah, brown cottages with their own porch and rockers, various outbuildings, piles of firewood lying in a ring of wood chips, a garden cart full of fresh linen, a dock with boats and canoes, everything looking as if it had been lifted from a sepia postcard circa 1888—it's all very typical of the classic Maine fishing camp, an institution I've some affectionate familiarity with and would very much like in the coming years to have more.

A Maine fishing camp! The state that's given American culture the lumberman, the lobsterman, the Maine guide, has also given it this: the camp in the woods where the trout bite even faster than the black flies, the salmon leap into your canoe of their own volition, the griddle cakes come stuffed with blueberries, the loon calls at night, the moose bellows, and you sleep soundly under thick wool blankets even in July. I've fished several over the years, and find not only do they match up remarkably well against their stereotype, not only do they offer one of the most reasonably priced fishing experiences to be found anywhere, but they seem to be the kind of places where stories happen, and there's no higher praise in my vocabulary than that.

The first one I fished was Weatherby's up on Grand Lake Stream back in the '70s. I remember one night after dinner everyone congregating on the lawn to watch a guest cast with the latest marvel: a rod made out of graphite fiber. Next day, going out with an old guide in a Grand Lake Stream canoe, I timidly mentioned I preferred fly fishing only. "Fine with me, young fella," the guide said, then promptly reached into his bait bucket and slapped a shiner on my Mickey Finn. A few years later, married now, I took my wife and baby daughter to Kidney Pond in Baxter State Park at the base of Mt. Katahdin—the old Colt family camp, operated as a modest lodge. Celeste and I spent our evenings fishing (in an Old Town wood-and-canvas canoe) a hundred yards offshore from our cabin, listening to our sleeping baby through the crib monitor we'd brought from home. On that same trip, fishing dry flies, I let my line trail out the back of the canoe as I paddled to a new spot—and was promptly arrested for trolling by a hidden game warden, despite the fact that what I was "trolling" was a size 24 Black Midge.

Maine fishing camps fell upon hard times in the '80s, partly due to changes in logging practices (more tote roads, clear-cuts, aerial spraying), and partly due to their own lack of foresight. One of the *big* routines at fishing camps has always been having trout for breakfast, and too many camps were too slow in getting behind catch and release. Now they are starting to see the light; Stan Milton, for example, is one of the most vocal proponents of catch and release in the state. It's paying off, with bigger fish, more fish. In our cabin at Lakewood was a creel census conducted over the course of a decade. In the first year there wasn't *one* legal salmon released by anyone; in the latest year, they *all* had been released, and the fishing had improved enormously.

The camps still have problems, including the fact that logging roads go everywhere now, and any fisherman with an ATV, a DeLorme atlas, or a Magellan navigation system can find their way to water the camps once pretty much had to themselves. You have to wonder how much longer sports will pay for ambience alone, when there is no longer this de facto kind of privacy. Against this is the fact that the fishing-camp concept is environmentally friendly, limiting the numbers of fishermen and keeping them under some kind of watchful control.

Checking in at a fishing camp is always part of the ritual. Buying a three-day license, asking about the fishing, scanning the logbook to see who's caught what, buying some locally tied streamers, adding in some postcards, getting meal times set. On the boat ride over Stan told us the fishing was slow, but Sue, his wife, assured us it was splendid, so between them they had prepared us for anything.

We picked up a picnic lunch out in the kitchen, then went back to our cabin, got our fishing duds on, headed down to the river—and right into our second fast story of the trip. The Carry Road follows the river, but we managed to take a wrong turn and before we realized it, we were pretty well lost. This was vexing, and seemed somehow part of an initiation—the land blindfolding us, spinning us three times around. Finally, after growing impatience on both our parts, we spotted Pond-in-the-River below us through the forest and sheepishly made our way down to where the river empties into the pond in what is called, none too promisingly, Chub Pool.

Whoever named Rapid River wasn't kidding . . . it really scoots along, a staircase of boisterous rapids . . . but where we intersected it the water broadens and slows. The salmon were rising when we got there and it took us a while to figure out how to connect with them, not so much the flies they were taking (small gray midges), but where to best position ourselves in the water. Unlike most salmon rivers in Maine, here the landlocks remain in the river all summer long, but they really get moving in the fall, joined by migrants up from the pond—a movement it's most enjoyable to witness, since it's seldom in New England we see the seasonal migration of fish you get in a place like the Pacific Northwest, landlocks being the closest we come to an actual bona fide run.

They're dignified-looking fish, landlocks—light silver and lightly spotted—and seemed compelled to jump primarily because they're shaped for jumping, with the muscular kind of leanness you see in world-class pole vaulters. A little one will jump five or six times before you bring it in; a thicker one, three or four times, but with a slower, more graceful kind of panache, the vaulter at the moment of releasing her pole and arcing that final millimeter over a barely trembling bar.

Sometimes in autumn spawning brook trout migrate up the Chub Pool, and for a moment I thought I had one on, but it turned out to be one of the huge and eponymous chub, just red enough around the gill area to have me fooled when I saw it deep in the water. I landed it, then waded over to the low, ragged isthmus that divides the pool in half, found a flat rock, and took a contemplative rest (reading Rich that night, I discovered this was her favorite spot to go smelting in the spring, allowing her to dip her net in either channel). Out in the deeper part of the pool, Tom, as usual, was testing the limits; he's gone as far as he can, I decided, but then, with a magician's graceful flourish, he reached into his vest for a gadget I didn't know he had; a collapsible wading staff. Extended, it gave him just enough purchase to keep going across the pool.

If you travel even a few feet into the brush here you'll come across reminders of the old logging days, thick rusty cables wound around cedars or peeling yellow birches, making it seem as if giants who had once fished here had left their set lines behind. In reality, they were cables used in getting the pulp downriver each spring; once the logs reached Pond-in-the-River they were collected in huge booms and towed across the water by ungainly vessels called Alligators.

> Alligators are built like barges, flat and rectangular, but they have a huge steel cable running from a winch in the bow. The anchor is dropped, the winch unwinds as the Alligator runs backward to the boom, and hooks on; then the winch winds up the Alligator to the anchor, trailing behind her the boomful of pulp wood which is her business to move from the Head of the Pond to Pondy dam at the foot. . . . The crew looked like any gang of men going about a routine job, except they were a little shabbier, a little more nondescript, a little less arresting than any bunch of road menders I ever saw. There wasn't a plaid shirt in the crew. Tied like a baby's bonnet under the chin and tucked into the shirt at the back of the neck was a bandanna handkerchief, or, failing that, just an old piece of flour sacking. On top of that was the hat proper, which might be a cheap felt, a visored cap, or a battered derby. They didn't even do the job with dash. They just walked apathetically up and down the logs, boring holes, driving pegs and fastening ropes. People who do things well almost always do them without flourish.

A tough, backbreaking job, pulp driving was, and though Rich could romanticize it at times, her eye was too honest not to see it plain.

I thought about this as I sat there watching Tom catch salmon. I thought post-industrial kinds of thoughts, trying to imagine how all this had looked during those years, finding, surprisingly, that I could do this without much trouble. It can be one of the charac-teristic notes when you fly fish New England in autumn—that between old stone walls and collapsed mills and washed-out dams you feel like you're fishing over the ruins of Rome. That's a com-forting feeling in this day and age, thinking the dreck we ourselves pile skyward might, in time, come to have the same kind of wist-ful burnish those rusty cables have taken on, our own era, like the eras before it, tucked to sleep beneath the trees.

Would Louise Dickinson Rich recognize her woods if she came back today, fifty years after she last lived here? On the sur-face, yes. Her house, Forest Lodge ("From the outside it's not a bad little house—a low building with a porch and an ell, set on a knoll with a view up the river toward Pond-in-the-River") still sits above the boulders and rapids of a river she would have no trouble recognizing. Middle Dam is much the same, with its proud white caretaker's house set beside the lake, its garden with a tall fence around it to keep out deer and bears. Lakewood Camps is much the same. The Carry Road looks the same, though it's not old jalopies that bounce along it now, but moun-tain bikes and ATVs. The salmon and trout fishing is probably almost as good as it was then, and may very well soon be better, *if* the fish and game department stays the course with catch and release. The ridges, the views of distant mountains, the look and feel of the forest, the autumn foliage—on the surface, much remains just the same.

It's on the deeper level that things have changed here. The pulp operation of the '40s was a brutal enough process, but not terribly efficient, not when compared with modern industrial logging, with its clear-cuts and aerial spraying, its reliance on bulldozed roads, not free-flowing rivers. You have to wonder how long it will be before someone decides to play around with the dams; originally intended to provide heads of water for the log drives, they have served the Rangeleys well over the years, but in the future, who knows? Already plans have been floated to bury an enormous pipe along the Rapid River as part of a massive hydroelectric project. Second homes go up on Umbagog and the other Rangeleys as woodland is "harvested" and "liquidated." Powerful forces would like to make money out of the region, big money, and care not a whit for anything but making it pay.

What's changed the most, though, is the sense people bring to this place—the baggage we all carry now of knowing too much. Too much about what? About the threats that the last beautiful places in the world are subject to even in the best of circumstances, when their rareness and isolation alone are enough to make them targets. Fifty years ago this was a truly forgotten corner of the world; now, even on a casual visit like ours, you get the sense a garish spotlight is shining on the woods from the distance—not constantly, not even deliberately, but including it on each slow, inescapable sweep. Anyone who loves this kind of place, anyone who sought to make a life here, rather than feeling the sense of freedom that Rich felt, would inevitably feel threatened and somehow trapped. There are no malls here, of course. But in a mall kind of culture, the microbes are carried on the wind.

Gloomy thoughts? Yes, but I was trying to see things as Rich would, understand the differences of a half century measured by her own honest standards. She was quick to defend herself against charges of escapism, maybe too quick, since in a world gone mad escapism of her sort, a basic physical escape, is not necessarily such a bad thing. But this is much harder now, if not downright impossible. You duck your head, arrange your life quietly, and just because of this, the world seems to mark you out for extinction. "Happy the land that has no history," she wrote, quoting the old classic tag; perhaps, coming back now, she would find to her dismay that history has these last lonely places and the people who live there square in its sights.

For my own part, I had come to her woods to see if the land was worthy of being the stuff of boyhood dreams, and the answer to that is yes, even if some of the dream was now in the process of vanishing before my middle-aged and far-too-cynical eyes.

That night Tom and I walked over to the lodge before dinner, and, while we waited, browsed among the various announcements and articles tacked to the walls. One of these, from a newspaper only a few years old, was Louise Dickinson Rich's obituary. She died in her 80s, having moved to the Maine coast after her years in the woods and written about her new life there in another round of books. Whoever had done the obituary had done some research, found men and women who had known her in the Rangeleys, including Al Parsons, the woman who was the caretaker at the fishing camp, her neighbor and friend. Mrs. Parsons allowed as to how Louise was a remarkable woman, though too prone, in her view, to swallow the stories the lumbermen told her as the gospel truth. As the obituary writer hinted at but didn't quite say, hers had been a remarkably successful career, measured in her own terms—a writer who had not only captured the spirit of a unique place, but had managed to color that place with her own spirit so the two were forever twined.

Like any good writer, Rich wrote her own epitaph without meaning to:

> It seems to be that the thing you spend your life trying to build, if you would be whole, is not a bank account, or an unimpeachable social position, or success in any one of a

thousand lines of endeavor; it seems to me that the only thing worth having is a certainty of yourself, a complete confidence in how you will act under any circumstance, a knowledge of yourself. People who have this knowledge are people who've kept their edges intact, people with what I can only call *core*. . . . Here in this country I found the circumstance and conditions that will make a woman of me, if anything will.

In the center of this is her elegy: Louise Dickinson Rich, taken on her own humble terms, was a writer with core.

After dinner, Tom wanted to pay homage to a local heroine of his own: Carrie Stevens, the famous fly tyer, inventor of the Gray Ghost, who had lived at Upper Dam on the north end of the Richardsons. He'd bought his tying supplies along; what better way to honor her than by tying up some of her famous patterns? Me, I strolled down to the lake, stared out across the water toward the slopes of Metallak Mountain, which still held enough red and gold in its foliage that it glowed like an eastern sunset mimicking in muted terms the one just finishing in the west.

Surely this hadn't changed—the lap of waves on the rocks, the early stars, Cassiopeia and the Dipper. I walked to the water's edge, picked up a stone, skimmed it toward what was left of the color, listened as the last faint skips faded into blackness . . . then turned and walked back to the soft yellow light of our cabin, where, silhouetted in the window, Tom bent his head down over his fly vise, getting us ready for morning.

Last Time Out

A CERTAIN AUTUMN LIGHT, a particular October color, can be seen on the upper reaches of the Connecticut River in its purest form—a light it's difficult to find exact words for, but that it might be possible to roughly surround. There's amber in the base of it, a watery brown-gold that widens from the streaks left in the river by a weakened and softened sun. Amber, the preservative kind, as in amber wax, so the light has an everlasting quality, making the rocks, the banks, the trees glow with the kind of burnish things take on in their final moments, fooling you into thinking they're eternal the moment before they disappear.

On a dry, crisp kind of day, there's still a humid quality to it all—you might be submerged in the shallows looking up. The gray element comes from the upper slopes of the surrounding hills, a stain leaking down from an ancient tin bucket. The tinge of copper involves the sumac, the last maple leaves just barely clinging to their branches. Blue comes in, too, but a distant, remote blue, up high in the sky on the other side of the amber, so it seems to box in and emphasize this self-contained, timeless quality all the more. It's the kind of light that might bring you intoxicating happiness or unbearable sadness, depending on your mood, your age, the circumstances of your life. It's a light, a color, that a week earlier in the season is camouflaged by the brilliant foliage, and only becomes predominate when the leaves have fallen; it is *past* the peak of foliage, and yet represents in secret, with hardly anyone noticing, the very height of the autumnal tint, the moment when the season crests and nothing will ever be quite so beautiful again.

A light that seems to carry with it a message, a simple and important lesson, yet one that comes in a code so complex you could spend your life trying to decipher it and never even find the first letter. Certainly, he'd been staring at it long enough as it was—the whole morning practically, time when he should have been fishing. Working upstream of the island he had picked up a few small trout, and had every expectation of catching something larger in the pool that turned itself around in a lazy semicircle, then widened out toward New Hampshire—and yet, seeing this color, feeling it, there was no other response possible but to wade over to the island, find a flat spot in the sandy marge, lie back with his head on a driftwood stump, and try to come to terms with what the light was telling him, even if it spoke in tongues.

The correct light of solitude. A phrase came to him after all— he always felt much better with things named. What the phrase actually meant he wasn't sure, but there was a nice lyric ring to it, and he had learned a long time ago that words with a compelling rhythm could sometimes form a working substitute for truth. He felt his own solitude with more than usual strength today; happy with friends, with children, he didn't go fishing alone as much as he had when he was younger, and something nostalgic in the sensation went down well with the amber light. His was by no means of a gloomy disposition, but it was

241

undoubtedly a pensive one, and he had a tendency to see things with an October coloration even in July.

No one else was fishing this stretch of river. Driving north he hadn't seen any cars parked along the railroad stretch or the Trophy Pool, and even below the bridge to Colebrook, where there was almost always a spin fisherman, the river ran uninterrupted by anyone's hips. The island itself was a popular enough spot, at least during summer. The river rolled past a beautifully dark bank of pine, then hooked left in some shallow, ferocious-looking rapids that divided themselves around the prow of a steep island, with deep holding pockets along both sides. With the water at its lowest level of the season, the island wore a collar of very fine sand, just wet and yielding enough to record the hops, skips, and plunges of raccoons, muskrats, and deer.

The maples on the crest of the island were already leafless; after a summer of green, an autumn of yellow, the branches seemed sharp and startling, studs without sheetrock, a scraggly grid. Toward the Vermont shore the bankside trees gave way in a narrow portal . . . there was an old town hall, a field behind it of stubbled corn, a rusty tractor, a shallow tributary stream . . . and it was through this gap that the amber color poured in at maximum strength.

But he was drifting now, so lost in looking he'd neglected his theme. The solitude part. Well, there was the solitude of the writer, which was no cliché. The solitude of the fly fisher wandering through rivers in search of trout. The solitude of a puny mortal face to face with one of nature's big deals. Here the Connecticut was the longest river in New England, some four hundred miles of beauty free for the taking, and yet on a weekday on the far side of foliage season how many people were doing what he was doing—sitting there, watching it, trying to figure out one of its tricks. To him the river wasn't something glanced at in the course of the day, not a flat, boring gray interval crossed on a concrete bridge or an opaque haze seen from an office tower, but something he must sit down and stare at and consider as the biggest, most important fact in the small corner of universe he found himself occupying.

And he felt he was getting somewhere now. Not arrived, not on the verge of anything major, but making progress, with the solitude stuff and the color both. Fishing with one of his partners he may have seen the color, but not recognized it; alone, the color merged with something inside him and so became even more noticeable, until the amber lightened toward yellow and grew even softer, more diffuse, and yet with a subtle grain (it could have been that of well-sanded maple) that connected everything to everything else. It was the light the Connecticut wore when no one was watching, and it was precisely this feat, to see a river clear, free momentarily of any human tint, that was what he had been after all along.

Closing day. It's never become the distinct ritual opening day is, and yet to many fly fishers it's a much more significant event. Opening day in northern New England is a cold and inevitably empty experience, redeemed hardly at all by the fact it's your first time out. Elsewhere in the country, fishing seasons have become so flexible, with so many special exceptions, that opening day has lost its position on the calendar as a distinctly April kind of event. Opening day is supposed to bring thoughts of rebirth and regeneration, a renewal of vows, a fresh start, but the fishing is so poor then, the climate so wretched, that the mood of nature contrasts too ironically with the mood of the fisherman for any kind of harmony to take place.

It's different in the autumn—in autumn, the fly fisher's mood and nature's mood are inevitably in sync, and even more so if the fisherman is starting to get up there in years, so any autumnal note in the river finds its immediate echo in an outlook that's taken on the same kind of gentle bittersweetness. A good year, a season full of fish, friends, and stories, and yet it's almost over now, with only one last chance to make the connections that have become so precious—and how sweet everything becomes when seen with this realization.

The only analogy is to a love affair. The beginning can be lost in obscurity, a matter of glances and idle chitchat, hardly remembered, and yet the ending—well, the ending can be remembered for a very long time. To enter upon one of these affairs each year, the kind that takes up a good deal of your being, occupies many of your waking hours, puzzles you, confuses you, fills you suddenly with delight . . . to enter upon one of these knowing in advance it will all end at sundown on October 15 with no extensions makes you pay very close attention as the days dwindle down, so those last weeks are often the sweetest, the saddest, the most intense.

Almost everyone feels something of this in autumn, or how else could it have become such a metaphor, life simultaneously at its richest and most heartbreaking. The fly fisher feels this intensely, and this particular fly fisherman, the one still sitting there on the sandbar staring out at the river, his thermos of tea sending up wispy, hookah-like clouds of steam past his head, felt it with an extra, very personal intensity and had for many years.

When he was a boy his parents owned a summer house on a lake in what was then still country. They would go there October weekends, rake leaves, take walks, go fishing, and then on Sunday it always came time to leave. The boy never accepted this—that they had to abandon what was already most precious in his life, the shining water, the fragrant woods, the sky with its wind-driven clouds, the ready supply of exhilaration. As they drove down the lake road there would come a final moment when the lake was still in sight; sitting in the back seat, craning his neck, he would steal one last glance at the full expanse of water shining golden under the afternoon sun—and often see there, in the one small wedge of blue still visible through the window, a boat with a fisherman just going out.

Never had he wanted anything so badly—the freedom to do just that, go fishing in October on a late Sunday afternoon when the rest of the world was going back to the dreary suburbs. So intense was this moment that it became one of those you hear about and seldom actually experience: a defining moment, an instant when everything he wanted in life became peculiarly concentrated and clear. A life where he could somehow marry nature, be free of the barriers that walled him off—a life, to put it in simplest terms, where autumn was perpetual and he could go fishing forever.

He was up against that right now—the moment it became clear every year that, fish as much as he wanted to, it would never be forever. This saddened him, but he had been saddened many times before, and so it had become part of the cycle—a pleasant sadness now, without the torment he knew as a boy. All those years of fishing. All those trout and bass. The stories, the friends, the adventures. Minor victories and shattering defeats. The rivers, ponds, streams. The books he had written about them. All flowed from that moment in the car, that brief glance of longing back over his shoulder as his future receded into the distance and disappeared.

But that was the good news—that he could still wish for anything as passionately at fifty as he had at fifteen. It came over him in a wave, between one moment and the next, so he jumped up from the sandbar (anyone watching would have thought he'd been stung) and waded back out into the current, high stepping through the rapids, false casting furiously even before he decided where to aim. It often happened like that in October. The introspection leading toward boyhood, hitting a memory there, rebounding back again, springing him into instant life.

Against the island the rapids ran choppy and deep, but over toward Vermont the river widened over a sandy bottom into a good-sized bay. Not a spot he would have tried ordinarily, but it was autumn, and almost any odd corner was worth a shot. The browns moved a lot in autumn—they were spawning, or soon would be, and the same was true of brookies. October 15 was a bit early for spawners (which is why it was closing day in the first place), but it had been a cold month, and the slow sandy backwater was definitely worth a few casts.

If his fly ever had a name he'd long since forgotten it—a foil-wrapped streamer with a long black shock of hackle guaranteed to make any spawner mad. He fished it near the seam that divided fast water from slow, still not convinced there could be anything in the backwater proper, and only after a half hour went by without a hit did he start casting closer to the bank. Hardly more than a foot of water covered the sandy bottom here, and it was littered with the kinds of things that regularly find their way to shallow backwaters: waterlogged branches, a scum of old leaves, broken corn stalks, a sunken tire. For one impressionistic moment it reminded him of those old Walt Kelly drawings of Okefenokee Swamp, and it was only the bright clattery rush of water to his left that reminded him he was fishing for trout and not largemouth bass.

Three casts, four casts. He took a few steps downstream, aimed for where the Vermont bank jutted out just far enough to add some vivacity to the sluggish flow. In the current, trout hit hard and fast, and so he wasn't quite prepared for a softer kind of take; the streamer was swimming sideways when something picked it up and carried it on back toward him, as if wanting to save him some stripping, help him out.

The lifting motion brought the trout's snout and gills clear of the surface. A *huge* fish—a brown trout judging by its color— and the split seconds that followed this realization were taken up by all the usual clichés. Surprise, shock, the frantic tightening— and then the sudden overwhelming disappointment as the trout, wearying instantly of the game, dropped the package and swam free.

A five- or six-pound trout by the look of it—easily the biggest fish he'd ever seen in the river. That his hunch had been correct didn't do much to assuage the pain; that the fish had simply let go, through no fault of his own, didn't help much either. He'd lost the kind of trout that comes only once a decade, the clock was reset again, and it would undoubtedly be another ten years before he had a similar chance.

What to do with this kind of disappointment? Check your barb, check your tippet, blow on the streamer for good luck, send it back out searching once again. For he had another hunch: if there was a big brown male cruising the shallows, then it was reasonable to expect an equally big female. And this is exactly what he found, sort of. A few casts later another trout took hold, and this time, rather than swimming straight for him like the first fish, it turned downstream and hooked itself firmly in the jaw.

A brook trout this time, a female about fourteen inches long, with a color not much different from the muted gray-green of the bankside shrubs. A few casts later he hooked another brookie in exactly the same spot, a male, about the same size, and yet a dozen times more fiery, with the kind of flaring redness you see in tanagers and maple leaves and hardly anything else, at least here in the north.

Between them, the three fish gave him a lot to think about. They were obviously fall spawners, ready to strike at whatever came along, so there was very little skill involved with their capture. If anything, he felt more than a little abashed. This sandy backwater formed the trout's bridal suite, the honeymoon cottage, the inner seraglio—the sanctuary an October 15 closing date was meant to ensure. Here, in all innocence (well, semi-innocence; he'd cast there in the first place prospecting for spawners) he'd stumbled into it, and rather than continue any further he turned now and, all but blushing, tiptoed back toward the Vermont shore.

The trout had taught him something, no doubt about that. Here between the light and his memories he'd been indulging himself in a *temps perdu* kind of mood, seeing everything as mellow and finished, with a patina of regret that went down well with October. But this was entirely too anthropocentric of him, too narrow, because not ten yards from the island on which he lay daydreaming, rebirth and regeneration and renewals were all going on in full force, so it was spring there, and not just metaphorically—those fish weren't hanging around to give him a frisson of guilt, but planning their species' continuance, actively working at it, swimming around and around and around as if to spin the water to their genetic purpose.

It took a while before the heavy sense of intrusion left him and he began to see the backwater in a different light. That trout could still teach him things, shake up his humanity, point him where to look for the new lessons anyone his age needed if they were to continue growing was very good news indeed. The great cycle of life—there it was in action; he needed to keep a closer eye on it, factor it more into his autumnal mood, realize nature's clock didn't stop sweeping just because the small hand was brushing past the ten. He'd been looking at October 15 all wrong; if it was closing day for the fishermen, it was opening day for the trout. He'd imagined an October composed of wistful sadness; he'd neglected the October composed of exuberant lust.

Time, as a philosopher would put it, for lunch. He walked back through the empty cornfield to his car, folded his waders down around his waist, shook himself like a wet retriever, spread his anorak on the seat, got in. Colebrook in New Hampshire was the closest town, but small as it was it seemed too much like a metropolis, and so he drove the extra few miles to Bloomfield in Vermont, which hadn't been a metropolis or anything like it since the log drives at the turn of the century.

A pleasant enough drive. He had thought perhaps the amber color was entirely confined to the river, but he could see now it was much wider and more diffuse, and rather than holding over a definite channel it colored barns and farmhouses and meadows all the way up the first range of hills. He also realized he had seen this tint before, in the work of English watercolorists of late Victorian times, those who often set their landscapes in November, seeing as they did with the haze of knowing that the pastoral life, their subject, was coming to an end. It wasn't November yet, but no matter—the same mood was in the air.

A few miles north up this road a sign announced that you had crossed the 45th parallel—a sign that always seemed to him of a remarkable double significance. First, to think that northern Vermont was just as close to the equator as it was to the North Pole; second, that already, at 45 degrees one split second north, there was not only a definite northern flavor to everything, but a *high* northern flavor, at least late in fall. The Connecticut ran south, while its valley seemed like a gap up which everything poured toward the arctic, so the river alone escaped the latitude and its implications, but nothing else in the land could.

DeBannville's sits on the highway just back from where the Nulhegan enters the Connecticut. It's typical of what country stores have become, here and elsewhere—outlets for lottery tickets, sugar, fat, salty things, and six-packs—and yet with enough chain-saw oil, fishing lures, and axes that it still retains something of the old kind of flavor. Attached on its ell is a small restaurant that serves burgers and fries; a greasy spoon, strictly speaking, but it has one feature that places it in the very forefront of American restaurants: no one cares when patrons come in wearing muddy waders.

Midafternoon now, he had the place to himself. The waitress doubled as short-order chef—an older woman, French, the *mémere* kind that looked as if she would be good at a motherly kind of clucking. She grilled up his hamburger, brought it over with a tall glass of ice water, then stood there staring at the sunshine that streamed through the screen door.

"Slow day," the fisherman said.

And yes, she did cluck—and followed it up with a phrase in French that was so soft he couldn't catch it.

He took a swallow of the water. "Looks like winter is coming."

She faced the door. Oblivious to him now, griddled in sunshine by the screen, she ran her hand back through the gray of her hair, and said something so odd, so off the turn of their small talk, he ended up thinking about it the rest of the day.

"Winter? Oh no," she said, again with the same softness. "It *mustn't* come, not this year."

"I'm sorry?" he said, obtuse.

She turned, blinked to see him, smiled at him like he was a little boy. "We have a very nice maple pie."

He thought about it on the way back to the river—how much force she put into the simple phrase, how odd the construction was with that prim, old-fashioned *mustn't*. May as well insist the earth stop spinning, poor woman. The sky remained soft in the east, swollen with autumnal haze, and yet to the west the clouds seemed hard and suspiciously silver, as if they had already been rolled and coated in December.

Time enough for one last pool. He parked at the airstrip, then pushed and swatted his way down through the briars until he was abreast the sandbar that formed one side of the pool. Up high on the New Hampshire bank the small brown cabin was all shuttered and closed; there was no sign of his friend who, in springtime, would stand there pointing out the trout.

He waded through the easy, slack water until he came to the tail of the pool, then veered out gradually into the heavier current, letting the force of it slide on past his hip. Halfway to the river's center he heard a sound that lay between a flute's airy whistle and a whirligig's frantic click, turned his head around and quickly ducked as two mergansers came racing downstream, their red heads extended as if each were trying to beat the other across an invisible line.

A good hatch of olives was in progress at the tail of the pool, just as he had hoped (olives being the most reliable insect emergence of the year). Little wispy things, olives, more like miniature stick figures than full-bodied bugs, dabbed together with the minimum amount of gluten; easy to imitate if you're comfortable fishing minutiae. The smaller the fly, the less there is for a trout to dislike—a theory he had always found to be true.

There were lessons here, just as there had been further upstream—the same lesson, only compressed into a tighter cycle. Fall, winter, spring, summer. The olives packed all these into the course of a single day, and this was the spring part, the miraculous regeneration going on in airy swarmings right before his eyes.

The trout rose like it was June, too—busy little sips, as if someone underwater was sticking up a thumb and stirring the surface in quick clockwise swirls. He aligned himself with the current, fussed out some line, then let the fly drop just to the inside of the closest trout. It came up for the midge and missed . . . the fisherman, in striking, skipped the fly backward . . . and a trout he hadn't seen darted out from behind a rock, curled his flank around the fly in that endearingly protective gesture trout can make, then plunged toward the bottom with the midge firmly centered in the small bull's-eye pocket of its upper lip.

And as the trout (a rainbow, a rare one so late in the fall) gambols and prances around the high maypole of the uplifted rod, perhaps it's time to discard the transparent pronoun that has just barely divided this fly fisherman from me. It's a rhetorical trick, after all—borrowing the kind of distance grammar can sometimes lend—but not a shabby one. I was trying to see things with particular clearness this last time out, and for a while this kind of transference can help.

But not now. Here at the end of a season and a book it's as good an occasion as any to explicitly link what at times have seemed separate entities: the writer and the fisherman. "Yield who will to their separation," Frost puts it, "my object in living is to unite my avocation and vocation as my two eyes make one in sight." And these two halves *are* here, or should be, as soon as I pull the knot tight with a few brief words.

Why would a novelist bother to write about fishing? Chekhov in *The Seagull* has Nina marvel that the famous Trigorin would spend so much time along the river. "And is it not wonderful that a famous writer, the darling of the public, mentioned daily in the papers, with his photograph in all the shop windows, his books translated into foreign languages, should spend his whole day fishing and be delighted because he has caught two chub." Yes, wonderful indeed, not just for celebrities, but for those humbler, more obscure writers (though I bet I could outfish the vain and cynical Trigorin any day of the week) who find almost as much solace in fishing moving waters as they do in trying to capture moving character, or pinning down, if even for a moment, a secret or two about fate.

Fly fishing for me, as for most everyone who does it, is a welcome break from the daily grind. A baker, a master, someone who loves his craft, still knows moments when the hot oven, the demands of his customers, the very texture of flour and salt become unbearable irritants against his overworked nerves; he finds, in fleeing to the river, relief in facing nothing more vexatious than the vagaries of trout. So too with the writer of fiction. After a while he's had enough with words, enough with plot, enough with the long hours sitting bewitched, bothered, and bewildered at his desk, and it becomes of the utmost importance to concentrate on another matter entirely. Fly fishing, in this respect, is my booze, my womanizing—my strong avocational defense of my weak vocational flank. And it's exactly this transference that accounts for the intensity with which I pursue my sport; to balance the prolonged kind of concentration writing demands, you have to place something of comparable demand on the opposite side of the scale. Tolstoy pursued peasant girls, Nabokov chased butterflies—a writer's passion, off duty, can be an odd and terrible thing.

An understandable enough motive, fishing to get away from it all, known not only by writers and pastry chefs but garage mechanics and insurance executives, history teachers and nurses. But what gives it an added twist is that in my case when I'm out on the river I'm not only a novelist at leisure, but an essayist who sometimes writes about fly fishing, and this brings a portion of my vocation with me, so often I'm looking as hard for the right words on a river as I am back at home.

I've always thought the reasons for this are fairly straightforward, so much so that perhaps I've never bothered to spell them out. I write about fly fishing because I enjoy writing about delight; because in this day and age, when the worth of a novelist is still measured by how well he or she catches our despair, a fiction writer is not often called upon to write about simple happiness, and I'm determined to seize the chance when it comes. I enjoy writing lyrically, the old way, where the rhythm of words seeks to capture the rhythm of what they describe, and rivers lend themselves perfectly to this kind of treatment. I enjoy writing, not specifically of nature (for I find my eyes are too large and greedy to do this with any patience) but the stage nature performs on—of landscape, moving water, weather, sky, hills, and terrain.

And it's an odd thing. To the rest of the world writing fiction and writing about fishing seem totally opposite endeavors. "You write about *fishing?*" someone will say, in praising a collection of short stories. "You write *novels?*" someone will say, in praising your fishing essays. After a while you come to anticipate the little sneer that decorates the question mark, the upturned eyebrow, the slow confused shake of the head, as the person pigeonholes you as, in the first case, a redneck hick, or, in the second, a highfalutin intellectual.

Yes, I do both, find the rivers I fish in fact merge with the rivers I fish in imagination; watery metaphors are all-inclusive—they flow back around on themselves and merge.

For when you think about it, writing fiction and fly fishing for trout have much in common. Both are difficult (done right), both require long apprenticeships, both involve much patience, the capacity to withstand disappointment and failure, a healthy dose of skepticism, a certain daring, a sense of being part of a long and continuous tradition. Both, most of all, are honest and sincere attempts to come to terms with the world, make sense of it, if only for the length of a paragraph or one heartbreakingly golden yet all too perishable afternoon.

This is my third book on fly fishing—I don't think there will be a fourth. What they make up, taken together, is a record of three fishing seasons over the course of fifteen years, or rather *one* season in the life of man—a long one, extending from late youth to late middle age, the vital years of a person's prime. Together, they form a history of passionate involvement, an auto-biography of small delights, and it seems to me in finishing this third book that I've gone as far with this theme as I should.

This realization has something to do with the autumnal mood I tried so hard to recreate earlier, the light that, as I fished those olives, remained so pronounced. As a man nears fifty he can become too conscious of that light. Everything takes on a burnish, a retrospective glow, and it becomes harder to find that vernal kind of brightness that makes you want to throw your hands up and shout in sheer delight. Your eyes begin noticing how the pines all seem to be dying from roadside salt or acid rain; you see the houses going up too close to the river, the wanton disregard for all you hold dear; the fishing doesn't seem quite so good anymore; rapids you would have pushed aside in disdain only a few years ago now seem dangerous; the river, in little ways, seems out to get you. If you're lucky, there's still enough boy in you to bull past this sunset kind of vision, but it takes effort now; it's not something your genes do instinctively on their own.

October 15 is an appropriate date against which to cease and desist, not only to protect the river and its young, but to protect the youthful vision these books have tried to reflect. Yes, maybe someday it will be good to write of late season in a fly fisher's life, link it naturally to what's come before, but somehow I don't think so—what I have to say about rivers is largely finished. I say this in full and guilty consciousness of all those subjects I've never had time to write about at length. Swallows, for instance, the fly fisher's bird. Smallmouth versus rainbow, which fights harder. How wonderful food tastes when eaten beside moving water— the delights of a fishing lunch. Casting for gulpers in our local pond. My heretical theories on rods and tackle. My first striper. Which fishing writers have meant the most to me and why. Fishing with worms. All these and more I could have some fun with, and yet that October 15 date looms in finality and I realize there's no time.

This brings it back to what any fly fisher feels as the season runs down. So many stories yet to tell! And so many places left to fish! I'd like to go back to the Yellowstone again, early in the season when you can expect a good cutthroat on every cast. I'd like to fish the coastal rivers of British Columbia and then continue on up to Alaska, preferably on float trips, so the fishing is right there every moment of a long northern day. Explore alpine lakes up and down the Rockies. The smallmouth waters of Quetico-Superior, a canoe trip with my family. A week or two on the classic English chalkstreams, especially the Kennet, since it's along its banks where my parents first met each other in

World War Two. I'd like to go to Argentina and Chile, dust off my high school Spanish, catch trout under volcanoes. And Labrador, since I'm being ambitious—those landlocked salmon and brook trout rivers of the true north. Given time, I'd like to return to the lochs of the Scottish highlands, with my kids this time, show them that high lonely country that speaks to something in my imagination in an intense way no other landscape can match.

Thus, my wish list. Probably most of these places will always remain there, rivers to daydream about and keep alive in the wanting, even if my bank account, my health, or the vicissitudes of fate keep me from ever visiting them in person. There are places close to home I would like to fish, too. In Vermont, I'd like to think I could return someday to a revitalized Battenkill, or a Waits that was treated as the treasure it once was and could be again. In Massachusetts are those stripers that run off the Merrimack—why have I waited so long to find out what *that's* all about? In Maine, I'd like to visit more of the old-time fishing camps, get a better sense of the vast northern forest. And, for that matter, there are mountain ponds and upland streams right here in the hills that surround my home I've always wondered about but not yet explored.

But most of all, forming the dependable foundation on which these fancies soar, I would like to think I have many seasons left on my beloved Connecticut, running purer now than it has in a hundred years. Days like this one, for instance, when its beauty manifests itself in a guise I've never seen before, so it could be an entirely new river superimposed over my familiar one, needing this trick of light for me to see it clear. Watching it, very conscious of every surge and ripple, I caught four more trout at the tail of the pool, and the fish were still rising when I decided it was time to quit. The amber remained as pronounced as it had been in the morning, and I wanted to leave while it was still in place, take away with me the illusion that the river would run beneath the color all winter, preserved and protected by that pure crystal palace of autumnal light.

Facing a long drive home, tired, saddened, but no more than I should be, I reeled in my line, carefully distributing it with my finger so it lay even on the spool, knowing it would rest undisturbed there until spring. I was reaching to take down my rod when a fish rose ten yards in front of me—a good one judging by the thick way the ring crested, much better than the little brookies I'd been playing with downstream. I looked at my watch, then up at the sun, which was still ten degrees above the horizon, stalled in the wide bar of its own yellow warmth . . . took light and fish and mileage into consideration, decided it really was time to quit, started toward the bank, then quickly turned and shoved myself back into the current for one last cast.

One last cast! That's the fly you should use if you want to catch the spirit of this sport—the fly called hope. It filled me now, just as completely, with just as much exhilaration, as if the river had lifted me up on its back and transformed me into the same surging mix of hydrogen and oxygen it consisted of itself. I felt a gratitude so strong it all but made me sob . . . that so deep in autumn I could still feel the gift of such joyous exuberance . . . and at the same time a whole list of demands raced through my wanting—not the greedy kind, but the kind that are part vow, part prayer, part command, part supplication, and together make up a man's undiminished, unquenchable appetite for life.

One more time into the current, the force of it on my waist. Once more the feel of spray kicking up off my waders, flying in my face, making me laugh. Once more the magic bend and flex of a well-designed rod. One more sunset, slow and soft there in the west. Once more that precious hour before the light disappears. One more rise, slow and dimpled. One rainbow more, leaping wildly. One brown more, pensively gorgeous. One brookie more, skittering about. One hatch more one strike more one surprise more one victory more and below and through and around all these the most vital thing enduring thing now and yesterday and tomorrow and forever one river more one river more one river more *one river more.*